W9-ACB-806

COUNTRY WITHOUT A NAME

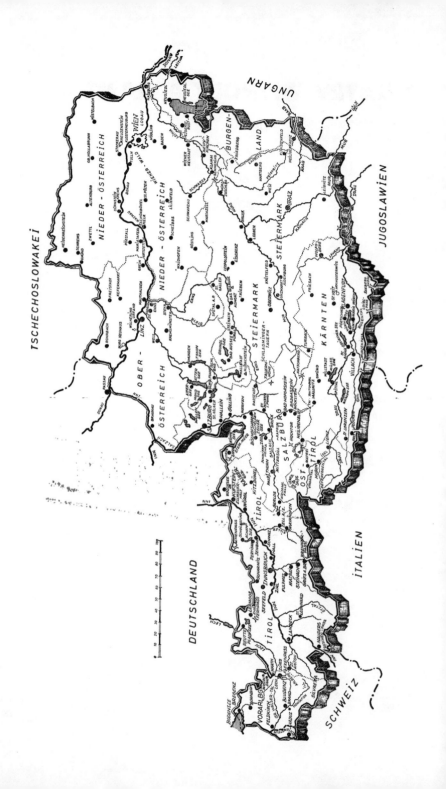

COUNTRY WITHOUT A NAME

Austria under Nazi Rule

1938-1945

WALTER B. MAASS

Frederick Ungar Publishing Co.
New York

Burg.
DB
99
.M3

WITHDRAWN

Copyright © 1979 by Frederick Ungar Publishing Co., Inc.
Printed in the United States of America
Designed by Stan Rice

Library of Congress Cataloging in Publication Data

Maass, Walter B
  Country without a name.

  Bibliography: p.
  Includes index.
  1. Austria—History—1938–1945.
2. World War, 1939–1945—Underground movements—
Austria. I. Title.
DB99.M3   943.6'05   78–4306
ISBN 0–8044–1553–6

This book is dedicated to those who gave their lives for Austria's independence.

Let's talk of graves, of worms and epitaphs;
Make dust our paper, and with rainy eyes
Write sorrow on the bosom of the earth.

SHAKESPEARE, *Richard II*

CONTENTS

PREFACE

When I left Austria in June of 1938, a tragic period, which was to last seven years, was just beginning. Many years later, in 1974, I became particularly interested in the Austrian resistance to Hitler and wrote a small brochure entitled: "Years of Darkness: The Austrian Resistance Movement, 1938–1945." I decided subsequently to describe more fully the events in Austria before and during World War II.

This book was written mainly for the American reader whose knowledge concerning Austria's fate under Hitler is very sketchy. The text is based almost exclusively on works published in Austria. I have tried to concentrate on the main course of events without going into too many details, not attempting to write a systematic history of National Socialism in Austria or of the opposition to it. The resistance consisted of many small groups, which were often completely destroyed by the National Socialist regime. It is impossible to relate their full story in a work of limited scope. I decided to mention only the major movements and some of their exponents; a multitude of minor episodes, tragic or heroic though they may have been, would tend to confuse the American reader.

Except for official newspapers and documents, there is very little literature on Austria from the German side. The Allies, on the other hand, almost ignored the Austrian question until the fall of 1943. When they finally occupied part of the country, they were ill prepared to handle the problems that turned up when the purely military actions came to an end.

I have only briefly touched on the conspiracy against Adolf Hitler in 1944, as this was basically a German enterprise, richly documented by many excellent books. I have therefore described only the events in Vienna on July 20, 1944, which of necessity were only a minor aspect of the plot. Ironically, the conspirators succeeded in Vienna while their coup d'état in Berlin failed, with disastrous consequences.

I thank the Archive of Documentation of Resistance in Vienna for its kind cooperation. My wife, Meta, was also of great help in the preparation of this work.

1
THE FALL OF
THE AUSTRIAN REPUBLIC

The Republic of Austria, founded at the end of World War I, ceased to exist on March 12, 1938, when it was invaded by German troops. For seven years it became a country without a name, a mere province of Hitler's Greater German Reich. Its disappearance marked Hitler's first aggression against a hitherto independent state and started the march of events that rapidly led to World War II.

How had all this come to pass?

Austria was the German-speaking centerpiece of the old Hapsburg monarchy that collapsed during the final days of World War I, in November 1918. The treaty of Saint-Germain (1919) established Austria's borders, with the clause that any political or economic union with Germany was prohibited. The victors of 1918 had no desire to strengthen the Reich that they had just defeated after a titanic struggle.

At that time many Austrians feared that their new little republic would be too weak to survive and therefore favored union (*An-*

schluss) with their larger neighbor, often somewhat wistfully called "our big German brother." This desire was born from economic considerations rather than from any great love or sympathy. Austria and Prussia—by then the strongest of the German states—often had been at odds. As recently as 1866 they had been at war. Their alliance during World War I was an uneasy one. The Germans considered their Austrian allies unreliable and inefficient. The Austrians disliked the Germans, whom they considered overbearing and arrogant. In fact, the last Hapsburg emperor, Charles I, made a clumsy attempt to dissolve the alliance and to conclude a separate peace with the Allies. German-Austrian cooperation during the war years was often far from harmonious. During the first decade after World War I, the Austrians became adjusted to their new republic, although pan-German feelings persisted and concentrated in a political party that called itself the "Greater German" (*Grossdeutsch*) party. There was also a lunatic fringe, the National Socialist Party (*Nationalsozialistische Deutsche Arbeiterpartei*—NSDAP), actually a subsidiary of the same organization in the Reich. Until 1932 it was of little consequence in Austria, although Adolf Hitler, the head of the German NSDAP, was Austrian by birth. In the last Austrian general election before World War II, in 1930, the voters gave the NSDAP, or "Nazis," just 2.5% of the total vote.

Austria's problems were both political and economic. During the postwar years, conflicts between the Right and the Left had multiplied. The former, mainly represented by the Christian Socialist Party, was Catholic and conservative, and it found its strength in the predominantly agrarian provinces. The Left, the Social Democrats, was strongest in Vienna—"Red Vienna," as it was commonly called. It was led by Marxists who liked to indulge in revolutionary slogans, but who were actually reformers. In 1929 the collapse of one of the major banks marked the beginning of the Great Depression in Austria. During the next years, things deteriorated to such an extent that by the winter of 1933 more than 316,000 Austrians were unemployed. It was during that bitter winter that Adolf Hitler became Chancellor of Germany.

The economic crisis and Hitler's rise to power gave the little Nazi party in Austria an unexpected impetus. Hitler always had declared that Austria belonged in the German Reich, that in fact all German-speaking people must be united. The idea itself was not quite new. An Austrian politician by the name of Georg von Schönerer had proclaimed a similar program as early as 1882. Hitler merely modernized and embellished the idea that Germans were a Nordic superrace, born to be the masters of Europe. The Führer had expressed these thoughts, including his plan for the future annexation of Austria, in his book *Mein Kampf* (*My Struggle*), long before he had the slightest chance to put them into practice. Unfortunately, few people took him seriously, least of all the statesmen of the Western democracies.

The Austrian Republic was troubled by growing unrest. From 1922 to 1929 the reins of government were mainly in the hands of Ignaz Seipel, a Catholic prelate and leader of the Christian Socialist Party. Seipel was a capable man who greatly contributed to the stabilization of Austria's economy. However, his views were reactionary and strongly opposed to socialist reform. His opponent on the Social Democratic side was Otto Bauer, a convinced Marxist who aimed at the establishment of a socialist state by democratic procedure. The conflict between these two men was symbolic for the political situation of the 1920s. The Social Democrats felt threatened and gradually established a workers' militia, the Republican *Schutzbund*. On the far Right a number of smaller militant organizations formed themselves into the *Heimatschutz* or *Heimwehr* ("home guard"), a sort of private army with strong fascist leanings.

On January 30, 1927, a minor clash between the *Heimwehr* and the *Schutzbund* at the village of Schattendorf in the Burgenland led to bloodshed. The Socialists were fired upon; a worker and an 8-year-old boy were slain. Three men were tried for the killings, but were acquitted by a jury. That sentence enraged the Viennese workers, and on the next day—July 15, 1927—a large, angry crowd demonstrated and clashed with mounted police. Some of the protesters set the Palace of Justice on fire. In the general confusion the police fired upon the crowds. The results were tragic: there were 90 deaths, including women, children, and 4 policemen, as well as close to 300 wounded. That bloody day had serious consequences. Seipel declared that no leniency would be shown to rioters. The Social Democrats countered by branding him as the "prelate without mercy," and 20,000 persons left the Catholic Church in protest. Seipel resigned in 1929 and died three years later.

One of his successors, Johannes Schober,[1] tried to establish a customs union with Germany in 1931, but the project was promptly opposed by France and her allies and had to be abandoned. The economic crisis increased and conflicts sharpened under several weak cabinets. In 1932, the chancellorship passed to Engelbert Dollfuss, a short man of an ambitious nature. His government, which included the *Heimwehr*, had only a one-vote majority in parliament.

In March 1933, Austria drifted into an authoritarian form of government; Dollfuss dissolved the parliament and established his own type of dictatorship. This was bound to aggravate the internal conflict with the Social Democrats, who had commanded 44% of the popular vote at the last election in 1930. At the same time the government faced growing agitation by the Nazis, who were constantly aided and abetted by Hitler's Germany. Dollfuss sought assistance from Mussolini, who was not yet disposed to allow the Reich to swallow Austria, and made an alliance with him in the summer of 1933.

The Nazis began to commit acts of terror, and in June 1933 Dollfuss decreed the dissolution of the NSDAP in Austria. A common front of all freedom-loving Austrians against Hitler seemed the logical consequence, but nothing of the kind happened. Mutual distrust was too great, and Dollfuss himself was now bent on authoritarian government, based on his own *Vaterländische Front* (Father-

[1] Schober served as police chief of Vienna from 1918 on and became Federal Chancellor in 1921 and 1929.

land Front), a shaky organization. Furthermore, his dependence on Italy forced him into close cooperation with the *Heimwehr*, which represented the Austrian brand of fascism. Suppression of all Leftist activities finally led to a workers' uprising on February 12, 1934.

The Republican *Schutzbund*, the Socialist militia, fought courageously for four days against far better equipped government troops. A general strike failed, and artillery shelling forced the well-defended public housing projects into surrender. The Social Democratic Party was banned, most of its leaders were imprisoned,[2] and nine members of the *Schutzbund* were court-martialed and hanged. These events drove the working class into sullen resistance toward the Austrian government at a time when every arm would have been needed to oppose the Nazis.

Abroad, the destruction of the Socialist Party diminished support for Dollfuss in the Western democracies but raised his stature in the eyes of his good friend Benito Mussolini. The Nazis tried to win new followers among the defeated workers, without any visible success. However, they managed to gain friends among some disgruntled politicians and civil servants whose loyalty toward the Dollfuss regime was questionable. Thus, in 1934 Austria's position had become precarious. Its very location between Nazi Germany and Fascist Italy made a truly independent policy difficult. Efforts to appease the Nazis remained fruitless. An Austrian Legion, about 15,000 men strong, had been organized in Bavaria with the clear intention to use it against the Dollfuss government. An intense campaign of subversion and terror, openly instigated by German propaganda, ensued. During May and June 1934 not one day passed without serious acts of sabotage committed by Hitler's Austrian supporters. In July 1934 they made an attempt to seize power by arresting the chancellor and his ministers. The coup d'état failed, but Dollfuss was assassinated and another short civil war erupted in Styria and Carinthia. The Nazis were defeated and

[2] Two prominent Socialists, Otto Bauer and Julius Deutsch, escaped to Prague. Bauer died in exile; Deutsch returned to Austria after World War II.

Mussolini moved Italian army units to his northern border. He had no desire to find the Germans suddenly as his neighbors. The events of July 1934 were a clear defeat for Hitler, who now decided to change tactics and undermine the Austrian state by different means. The Austrian Nazis were ordered to stop their terror, and a new ambassador, Franz von Papen, a seasoned diplomat with perfect manners, arrived in Vienna. The German press and radio, which had constantly attacked Dollfuss as a traitor and oppressor, suddenly evinced regret at his untimely passing.

The murdered chancellor was succeeded by Kurt von Schuschnigg, a man of integrity and reason and an Austrian patriot. Unfortunately, he failed to gain the full support of the population. The Socialist workers continued their silent obstruction, and nothing was done to win their cooperation. The Nazis remained the enemy within; their agitation was less visible, but their object—the destruction of Austria—remained unchanged.

In the meantime, the international situation was deteriorating. In 1934 Britain, France, and Italy were still united in their determination to protect Austria's independence. Two years later Mussolini, deeply embroiled in his Ethiopian adventure that led to a conflict with the Western democracies, turned toward Germany and the result was the Rome-Berlin axis. Hitler felt strong enough to occupy the Rhineland. France, as usual, did nothing. In England a tendency to appease dictators became a cornerstone of foreign policy. The outbreak of civil war in Spain strengthened the cooperation between Hitler and Mussolini as Spain became a proving ground for the fascist forces of Europe.

In July 1936, Schuschnigg tried to come to a better understanding with Germany by signing a treaty that confirmed Austria's independence as a "German state." Hitler made some minor concessions and declared that he would not interfere with Austria's internal affairs. That sounded like a success for Schuschnigg, but the heart of the matter was a secret agreement in which he promised political amnesty and cooperation with "representatives of the national opposition." That euphemism covered a number of respectable Pan-Germans[3] who pretended not to be Nazis. In practice, it meant that the unfortunate Austrians had to drag a Trojan horse within their own walls. Actually Schuschnigg, as he later wrote in his memoirs, hoped against hope to gain time by taking a flexible attitude.

The number of Austrian Nazi activists was probably not higher than 15%, but an equal number of Austrians were perfectly willing to follow their leadership. Dissatisfaction with economic conditions drove many persons into the arms of Hitler. In 1936 there were still about 350,000 unemployed people. In particular, many young men with academic degrees felt frustrated and looked with envy on Germany, where the rearmament program provided a growing number of jobs. The narrow, reactionary attitude of the Austrian government was another reason for the inner unrest. The regime was moderately fascist with a strong clerical undertone. Its Austrian patriotism was laudable, but its measures appealed more to the older generation of the middle class. It created little enthusiasm among young people, who were easily attracted by the grandiloquent Nazi slogans. The Nazi race theories were primitive, a Neanderthal nationalism, feeding on almost tribal instincts. Ironically, many of the believers were far from being Nordic supermen. The Austrians, especially the Viennese, have a strong Slavic element. Men with names like Reschny, Globocnik, or Proksch suddenly posed as Teutonic knights. First names borrowed from Richard Wagner's operas and Nordic mythology became fashionable. All this would have been merely comical, had it not fostered a particularly obnoxious fanaticism.

Anti-Semitism always had been latent in Austria. Its intensity greatly varied. Politicians of different persuasions had used it to their advantage; for example, Karl Lueger, the popular mayor of

---

[3] As a postwar political force, the Pan-Germans date from September 1920, when a number of national and provincial groups were consolidated in Salzburg to form the so-called Greater German People's Party.

Vienna from 1897 to 1907, for whom it was merely rhetoric, a "socialism for morons," as one of his adversaries called it. The early Pan-Germans invented racial anti-Semitism and supplemented it by hatred of Slavs, Socialism, and the Catholic Church. The Nazi ideology went one step further and used the Jew as the symbol of evil, the eternal antagonist of the noble Aryan. Consequently, the Jews were alternately damned as Capitalists, Socialists, Communists, Zionists, destroyers of German civilization, members of an international conspiracy, and despoilers of Nordic maidens. It is interesting to note that very similar accusations were raised against persons allegedly practising witchcraft in the sixteenth century.

Vienna had a strong Jewish influx during and after World War I, and there is no doubt that this increased anti-Semitic feelings. Times were bad, competition for jobs was fierce, and many of the new arrivals aroused a certain animosity with their strange behavior and idiomatic speech. Their business methods, moreover, were often resented by local shopkeepers. These newcomers had little in common with the native Jews, who were for the most part completely assimilated. However, fanaticism of any kind knows no logic. Many violent anti-Semites came from the alpine regions, where the number of Jews was negligible.

Perhaps the greatest strength of the Nazi movement in Austria lay in its efficient organization, which enabled it to infiltrate various government agencies. The danger already had been apparent in the attempted coup d'état against Dollfuss in 1934, when a number of police officers had turned out to be Nazi conspirators. During the following years that peril increased. Schuschnigg unknowingly weakened his position by appointing members of the so-called national opposition to high offices.

In the meantime Hitler got ready to strike. On November 10, 1937, he told his generals that actions against Austria and Czechoslovakia were imminent. His reasons were military and economic. His desire for a Greater Germany at that moment was less decisive than the wish to secure the Reich's southeastern flank. He was already planning his strategy for a major European war. Austria was only the first step. Economically, the small country was a great asset because of its large resources of iron ore and its impressive hoard of gold and foreign currency; in 1938, 44% of the money in circulation was covered by gold and currency reserves. By comparison, the Reich could only cover 1% of its currency by similar reserves. The Nazis were not slow in recognizing that a valuable hoard would fall into their hands if Austria were annexed.

In January 1938, the Austrian police raided the apartment of a certain Leopold Tavs, one of Schuschnigg's "national" appointees. Among his papers, a complete plan for the overthrow of the government was found. It was quite clear that this project was aided and abetted by Germany. In an atmosphere of nervous tension the German ambassador Franz von Papen suggested to Schuschnigg a personal visit to Hitler's mountain retreat in Berchtesgaden, only a few miles from the Austrian border. Schuschnigg expected a polite meeting of the kind that is customary among heads of state. But when he came face to face with the German dictator, he was bullied, blackmailed, and threatened with immediate invasion of Austria if he failed to bow to Hitler's ultimatum. Finally, he submitted, in the forlorn hope of saving at least a semblance of independence for Austria. Among the conditions he had to accept were an amnesty for all Nazi criminals, vast economic concessions, and —most important—two cabinet posts for Hitler's Austrian followers. The Department of the Interior, which controlled the police force, was given to Dr. Arthur Seyss-Inquart, a gentlemanly Pan-German who covered his treasonable plans with a show of reasonableness and religiosity. Schuschnigg, who knew him personally, was deceived by his accommodating attitude.

Encouraged by these developments, the Austrian Nazis now came out into the open. Their provocations were hardly opposed by the police, who felt uncertain about the situation. Schuschnigg desperately tried to hold the line. Belatedly he made contact with the leaders of the long-banned Social Democratic Party in hopes of uniting the majority of the population for Austrian independence. Finally, he announced an early plebiscite to decide the country's future. He figured, with good reason, that about 70% would vote for independence.

However, Hitler was not taking any chances. On March 10 he issued an ultimatum which forced cancellation of the plebiscite and subsequently the resignation of Schuschnigg and his government. The Austrian army would have resisted had it been ordered to oppose an invasion, but Schuschnigg preferred surrender to bloodshed. The whole apparatus of his government, long riddled with traitors, caved in. The unfortunate chancellor made a short speech over the radio which ended with the sentence: "God save Austria!" Then he went home and made no effort to resist when the Nazis came to arrest him. Only a few of his supporters managed to escape at the very last moment.

On orders from Berlin, Seyss-Inquart took over the reins of government. The President of Austria, Wilhelm Miklas, at first bravely refused to appoint him chancellor. In the end he too yielded to pressure and resigned. The German army marched into Austria, allegedly to prevent a civil war. In fact, there was no unrest and no danger of bloodshed. Afterwards, a forged telegram was issued to justify the armed invasion.

Hitler had timed his coup very carefully. France was once more preoccupied with one of its frequent government crises. The British government of Prime Minister Neville Chamberlain made no effort to intervene. Mussolini had decided many months before the event to abandon Austria. Only the Soviet Union and Mexico launched diplomatic protests.

The fact that the world accepted Austria's disappearance as an independent country as a *fait accompli* had serious implications. It indicated that treaties and solemn promises were without value if not strongly protected by armed force. Only a scant two years previously, Germany had declared that Austria's independence would be respected. Strategically, the *Anschluss* made the flank of Czechoslovakia crumble and gave Hitler easy access to southeastern Europe.

Furthermore, the *Anschluss* provided an example of how a government could be eroded from within. For years the Nazis had infiltrated every major government agency. Berlin was always perfectly informed about anything that went on in Vienna and could easily take countermeasures. Even the plans of the Austrian Chief of Staff were known to the Germans. They had forced Schuschnigg even prior to the invasion to dismiss Lieutenant Field Marshal Alfred Jansa, who had drawn up plans for Austria's defense. German agents had prepared lists of all citizens thought to be hostile to Hitler. No wonder that all these persons were arrested soon after the invasion with the greatest ease! Even in the highest government circles there were secretaries and officials who secretly worked for the Nazis. Schuschnigg's plan to run a plebiscite was known in Berlin within hours. A secretary who worked for Minister Guido Zernatto passed the still-secret information on to Berlin.

When the German troops poured into Austria on the morning of March 12, they were welcomed by large crowds in a jubilant mood. The photos of that triumphant entry were used by the German government as proof that everybody in Austria rejoiced at the invasion. Of course, many Austrians who felt very differently stayed home. The Austrian Nazis, quickly joined by a large number of fellow travelers and opportunists, controlled the streets and public squares.

Perhaps under the impression of that tumultuous welcome, Hitler decided to incorporate Austria into the Reich immediately. A formal proclamation of March 13 turned Austria into a German province. Soon even the name Austria disappeared, and for a time that new part of the Reich was referred to as Ostmark.[4] This too

---

[4] From an historical point of view, this was a misnomer. The authentic medieval name of Austria was "Ostarrichi." Ostmarken was in fact an old designation for the Bavarian marches.

soon fell into disuse. Eventually, Austria became a country without a name, divided into 7 *Gaue* (districts), including Oberdonau (Upper Danube) and Niederdonau (Lower Danube), that were ruled by *Gauleiter* (district leaders), all seasoned Nazis.

During the first weeks after the *Anschluss*, an Austrian Nazi government of sorts under the archtraitor Seyss-Inquart was formally maintained. The real power passed to the German *Reichskommissar* Joseph Bürckel. On April 10, a plebiscite confirmed the legality of the *Anschluss* post factum. To no one's surprise, more than 99% of the electorate voted "Yes" to unification with Germany. The population had been overwhelmed with Nazi propaganda, and a mere 12,000 people dared to vote "No." Although officially the vote was secret, there probably was some kind of control, and it took courage to cast a vote of protest. To assure the outcome, suspected adversaries of the new regime were barred from the voting in advance; a large number of them had been imprisoned right after the invasion. Besides, few people cared to vote against a *fait accompli.* Among the workers, few shed any tears for the fallen Austrian government; they figured that one type of fascism had merely been replaced by another. The Catholic part of the population was easily persuaded by Cardinal Theodor Innitzer, the archbishop of Vienna, that it was perfectly all right to vote for *Anschluss.* Innitzer, a naive and feeble man, honestly seems to have believed that his spineless attitude would gain advantages for the Church. He was soon to learn that he who sups with the devil must have a long spoon. A number of other personalities—among them the former chancellor Karl Renner,[5] a respected old Social Democrat—took a similar attitude. This was clearly not the hour for heroics.

Many Austrians who secretly disliked Hitler and all he stood for figured that the West had abandoned them and that one had to make the best of an unpleasant situation. The Treaty of Saint-

---

[5] Renner, born in 1870, became State Chancellor (*Staatskanzler*) in 1918 and resigned in 1920. From 1931–1933 he was Speaker of Parliament (*Präsident des Nationalrates*).

Germain (1919) had specifically banned any form of union between Austria and Germany. For years France, Britain, and Italy had paid lip service to Austrian independence as a cornerstone of European peace. When Hitler marched into Austria, they failed to take any action; in fact, Mussolini had become Germany's ally. Six months later, Britain and France were to accept the dismemberment of Czechoslovakia at Munich. This only reinforced the impression that resistance to Hitler was pointless. A great number of people began to feel that National Socialism was the wave of the future. Consequently, the more opportunistic joined the Nazi Party or at least one of its many subsidiaries just to stay on the safe side.

Another reason for the indifferent attitude of many Austrians was economics. For about eight years the population had lived with the specter of unemployment. The demoralizing effect of that situation was already visible in 1934 when the powerful railroad workers' union ignored the appeal of the Socialist leadership to strike against the Dollfuss government. The men were far too scared of losing their jobs to take such action. This had a decisive impact on the brief civil war between Dollfuss and the Socialists. Four more years of economic hardship under an unpopular government did nothing to improve the morale of the working population. At the same time, Hitler had drastically reduced unemployment in Germany. This was mainly achieved by the expanding armament of the Reich on its road to world domination. However, many Austrians did not care how such a reduction was achieved; they wanted jobs and paid little attention to anything else.

Finally, it must be remembered that long before the advent of Hitler the idea of *Anschluss* was favored by many politicians, particularly the Socialists. Of course, the Weimar Republic of that era bore no resemblance to the Third Reich. However, many persons who were far from being Nazis had a certain inclination toward a "German solution." Even Chancellor Schuschnigg, for all his fervent Austrian patriotism, motivated his surrender with his aversion "to spill German blood." All these factors contributed to the lack of moral fiber that a great many Austrians displayed during the first months after the German invasion. However, the impact of these actions would have been less powerful had they not been supplemented by another, more deadly weapon, the German secret police.

2
THE TERROR BEGINS

The German Secret Police, or Gestapo (short for *Geheime Staatspolizei*), had had its feelers in Austria for years. Immediately after the Nazi takeover, it went into action. At the very beginning, all Austrian police functionaries who were considered unreliable were dismissed and replaced by party members. This was comparatively easy, because the Austrian police had long been infiltrated. As early as 1934, when the illegal Nazi Party attempted to overthrow the Austrian government, a number of high-ranking police officers took part in the conspiracy. Four members of the Vienna police force were later executed and others—among them the chief of police, Otto Steinhäusl—sentenced to long jail terms. Steinhäusl, a well-known criminologist, was now appointed police commissioner of Vienna. The Germans had the Austrian police force under complete control before their adversaries realized what was going on. A great number of arrests were carried out by regular Austrian policemen who were either Nazis or afraid of losing their jobs and consequently eager to prove their loyalty to the new regime. In other cases the uniformed formations of the Nazis, the brownshirted SA and the blackshirted SS, were used. The former consisted of the rabble, while the SS was a well-trained elite guard whose ranks were filled with the most fanatical members. While Vienna was making preparations for Hitler's triumphal entry, the arrests began. Within a few days 76,000 persons were imprisoned. The jails were filled to capacity, and some school buildings had to be adapted to house prisoners. First of all, the whole top echelon of Schuschnigg's government and his Fatherland Front organization were put behind bars. Only a very few high functionaries like Guido Zernatto managed to reach the border during the night of March 11 before it was closed. From the next day on, rigorous regulations for obtaining exit permits were introduced and all borders were strictly controlled. The adversaries of the Nazi regime found themselves suddenly in a trap.

Schuschnigg himself made no effort to flee. He was at first interned in his home, then transferred to the former Hotel Metropol, the new Gestapo headquarters, where he was subjected to very degrading treatment. Originally the Nazis planned to put him on trial, but the idea was eventually dropped and he spent the next seven years in various German prisons and concentration camps.[1]

The more prominent political prisoners were shipped to the infamous camp at Dachau and treated in the most brutal manner. Among them were two men who were destined to play a big part in the Second Austrian Republic: Adolf Schärf, a Socialist, and Leopold Figl, head of a farmers' organization. The political detainees were only released after several years; many never returned, but died of ill treatment or starvation. Particularly tragic was the fate of Robert Danneberg, the former Secretary General of the Social Democratic Party. He attempted to escape from Austria during the night of the *Anschluss*, but could not pass the Czechoslovakian border because he had no visa. On his return to Vienna

---

[1] He narrowly escaped execution in 1945 and was liberated by the Americans. He emigrated to the US and became a professor at St. Louis University. Only in 1969 did he return to Austria; he died in Tyrol in 1977.

he was imprisoned. Danneberg was Jewish, and his party friends feared that the Nazis would ship him to one of their concentration camps. They tried to buy his freedom by offering a degree of collaboration to *Reichskommissar* Bürckel. These efforts were fruitless. Danneberg was transported to Dachau together with 150 politicians and writers. Eventually he died in Auschwitz. Another victim was Major Alexander Eifler, previously Chief of Staff of the *Schutzbund*, who survived years of imprisonment, only to die shortly before the liberation.

The majority of the arrested persons were not politicians, nor had they ever committed the slightest misdemeanor. They were simply considered hostile to Austria's domination by the Nazis, and this was quite enough to put citizens of a hitherto independent country behind bars. Many of them were prominent writers, actors, and artists, as Austria's intellectual elite had always rejected National Socialism. Many persons who were afraid of imprisonment and torture took their own lives, like the author Egon Friedell, who threw himself from a window when uniformed Nazis entered his house. It later turned out that they had no order to arrest him. The treatment of the prisoners varied. Some—mainly those who were Jewish—were released after some time with strict orders to leave the country as soon as possible. In most cases this also meant the loss of all their property. But a great many people disappeared for years into concentration camps. Those who for some reason were particularly hated by the Nazis had little chance to survive, since they were completely at the mercy of their tormentors.

All these measures had at least a semblance of legality, but in a number of cases not even the pretense of lawful procedure was preserved. Characteristic was the fate of General Wilhelm Zehner, a former commander-in-chief of the Austrian army. Two men entered his apartment, shot him, then placed a gun next to his body. The widow was told that her husband had committed suicide, and this was also the story published in the newspapers. The former Minister for Social Affairs, Odo Neustädter-Stürmer, was murdered while walking in the street. Another former member of Dollfuss' cabinet, Major Emil Fey, was found dead with his wife, son, servant and dog, all killed by gunshots. Here, too, suicide was the official explanation. All three men had played a part in the suppression of the Nazi coup d'état in 1934. The murders were probably acts of revenge by the SS.

During the first weeks following the invasion, mob violence was common. It was mainly directed against the Jews, who were completely defenseless as the police made no effort to intervene. They were forced to remove all signs and posters of the Fatherland Front while being abused by the mob. Cars belonging to Jews were simply confiscated, often by persons who had not the slightest right for such actions. Shops were looted and apartments ransacked. It became a popular entertainment to force Jewish storekeepers to deface their own shopwindows with anti-Semitic slogans. The German occupation troops took no part in such outrages.

While the adversaries of the regime were being suppressed in the most cruel manner, its Austrian supporters were wondering about their own future. The more moderate wing of the Nazi party had always figured that Austria would remain at least semi-independent with a local administration of its own. However, Hitler was averse to any kind of separatism. Seyss-Inquart, who had proved to be so useful a tool, got the high-sounding title of *Reichsstatthalter* (governor) but very little actual power. With the outbreak of the war he was transferred to Poland, later to the Netherlands.[2] Most others received only mediocre positions in various occupied countries. Of those who had led the underground struggle against Schuschnigg, only one, the sinister Ernst Kaltenbrunner, rose to prominence. We shall deal with his career later on.

A large number of German government officials were transferred to Vienna to set up a new administration. Until the fall of France, Joseph Bürckel remained the chief executive—at first *Reichskommissar*, then *Reichsstatthalter*. He always remained a foreigner in the occupied country. Even the Germans themselves

---

[2] Seyss-Inquart was hanged as a war criminal at Nuremberg in 1946 for the many atrocities committed under his reign in Holland.

admitted that their officials lacked tact and failed to establish any close relationships with the Austrians they were supposed to govern.

In the months after the *Anschluss,* an avalanche of laws and regulations descended on the bewildered Austrians, and Hitler, who was already planning his next act of aggression against Czechoslovakia, gave them no respite. Austrian currency, taxes, banking regulations, traffic laws—everything changed almost overnight. A flood of German entrepreneurs appeared to acquire Austrian factories at bargain prices. This was indeed easy, because all business enterprises belonging to Jews were available. Major firms were often simply confiscated by the Gestapo and transferred to "Aryans," particularly those with good connections to high party circles. In all other cases, the owner was forced to sell at a ridiculously low price. It was a great time for the vultures. More or less the same situation applied to homes and apartments as well as real estate. All these transactions increased German holdings in Austria enormously, a development which led to serious complications after World War II. Also, a great number of art treasures were confiscated under one title or another.

Of far-reaching importance were the changes in legal procedures. In June 1938 political offenses were withdrawn from the jurisdiction of the regular courts and turned over to so-called "special senates." They dealt with any act that fell under the loose definition of "subversion." This encompassed practically any criticism of the government, any action that could be considered hostile against the Reich. Often a relatively innocent remark was quite sufficient to get the accused a jail sentence. After the outbreak of World War II, listening to enemy radio transmissions became a serious crime. However, even the Gestapo could never prevent people from listening to foreign broadcasts, especially in the later phase of the war, when the hollowness of the German propaganda became apparent. Each special senate consisted of three judges, always reliable members of the National Socialist Party. Obviously, the prosecutor had to be an ardent Nazi, while defense counsel had at least to be approved by the party. It was understandable that such lawyers were extremely cautious in their arguments lest they too should find themselves in the dock. Nevertheless, some Austrian judges and attorneys tried to maintain strict professional standards. This took great courage, and many of the jurists ended up in prison. A typical case was that of Rudolf Granischstädten-Cerva, a lawyer who defended many members of the Resistance, until in August 1943 he himself was charged with membership in the Austrian Antifascist Liberation Movement.

Even if a defendant was acquitted, he was by no means safe from further persecution. The Gestapo could always rearrest him and send him to a concentration camp. In the first period after the invasion, the prisoners were usually shipped to the German camps of Dachau and Buchenwald. Later a similar camp was established at Mauthausen in Upper Austria near the provincial capital of Linz. It became one of the most feared concentration camps. In the 6½ years of its existence no fewer than 120,000 persons, citizens of many nations, died within its confines. Many inmates were worked to death or murdered in a quarry whose "staircase of death" acquired a sinister reputation. The prisoners were made to carry heavy loads, and the guards amused themselves by pushing them down into the ravine.[3]

Charges of high treason were not handled by the special senates but by the People's Court (*Volksgerichtshof*). This court can only be compared with Judge Jeffreys' bloody assizes in Britain (1685) or the French revolutionary tribunal of the Reign of Terror. We shall describe its activities in a later chapter.

A terrible impediment to future resistance was the fact that the complete archives of the Austrian police and of the courts fell into the hands of the Gestapo. Consequently, the latter was in possession of the names of all supporters of the Left, as these had been closely supervised during the Dollfuss-Schuschnigg era. When war broke out in 1939, all persons suspected of doubtful loyalty were arrested and made to join their leaders in the concentration camps. The few

---

[3] Today Mauthausen has become a shrine and contains memorials for the victims of many nations. A museum traces the history of the concentration camp.

old functionaries of the Social Democratic Party that remained unmolested, like the former chancellor Karl Renner and the highly respected former mayor of Vienna, Karl Seitz, were strictly watched and could survive only as inconspicuous citizens. The slightest suspicion concerning their activities could lead to immediate imprisonment.

The small Austrian army was immediately dissolved and those officers who were considered loyal to the fallen regime were permanently retired. The rest were incorporated into the German *Wehrmacht*. Naturally, Austrians were now subject to the German draft. In most cases the Austrian soldiers were divided among units from the Reich. The claim that during World War II Austrian troops were intentionally used for operations where high casualties were to be expected does not seem justified. It is true that their losses were extremely high; 171,000 Austrian soldiers were reported killed and 76,000 missing. This was an appalling bloodletting for a country with only 7 million inhabitants.

A similar purge was conducted on all levels in every government agency. The departments of Justice and Education alone lost 6,000 officials, who were promptly dismissed. Naturally, all Austrian diplomats who had loyally served their country were fired. Of those who had been active at embassies or consulates abroad, many remained in exile.

Indeed, few countries have ever seen so complete an upheaval as Austria after the *Anschluss*. The whole governing group was forcibly removed within days. This giant purge reached from the top echelons of the federal government to the burgomasters and district judges in small communities. The press, the broadcasting system, and all cultural organizations were immediately affected.

There were a number of other consequences which were only later realized. The city of Vienna ceased to be a capital and became merely one more large German city. From 1940 to 1943 it was even administered by a German mayor. At the universities all Jewish professors and those with an anti-Nazi reputation were dismissed from their jobs. Among them were scientists of renown like the Nobel laureates Erwin Schrödinger, Otto Löwi and Victor Franz Hess. Others, like the historian Oswald Redlich, president of the Academy of Science, resigned. The music of Gustav Mahler, the books of Stefan Zweig and Franz Werfel, the paintings of Oskar Kokoschka and Anton Faistauer were banned. Innumerable authors, composers, and scientists were forced to emigrate. As a result, the years of Nazi domination represented a nadir in Austria's cultural life.

3
COLLABORATION AND RESISTANCE

The events in Austria in 1938 cannot be classified as a revolution in the usual sense. The government was overthrown, the apparatus by which it had ruled was destroyed. A large number of persons were jailed, and even more went into exile. The disgusting mob scenes of the first weeks were characteristic of the most violent upheaval that had shaken Europe since the end of World War I. In 1918, returning army officers were abused and humiliated. In Germany, Hitler's rise to power had taken place among similar outrages, although with less violence than in Austria. However, all this only gave the appearance of revolutionary fervor; no social revolution occurred. In fact, the insurgents came from the same social background as their adversaries, predominantly from the lower middle class. The working man, as far as he represented industrial labor, took no part in the whole upheaval. The rather rigid class structure in Austria hardly changed, because the labor movement remained more or less outside of the event. It had not supported the Schuschnigg government, and it had little love for the Nazis.

The changes that took place occurred among the well-to-do and middle-class people. A considerable number of business enterprises changed hands, mainly because of the expulsion of the Jews. A similar change occurred in all fields where Jews were prominent, for example in the arts and sciences and among physicians, lawyers, and journalists. We have already mentioned government employees at all levels. The new arrivals were almost all Nazis, in some cases, Germans. At the beginning some Socialist city employees who had been fired by Dollfuss in 1934 were reinstated in an effort to gain labor support. However, since other old Socialists were savagely persecuted, that measure did not have too much effect. The "national revolution" in Austria can best be characterized by the French saying: *Ôte toi que je m'y mette!*" (Get out, so that I can get in). The social system remained the same. Basically, one form of authoritarian regime was succeeded by another one.

Obviously, a great number of people were bound to profit by this kind of local earthquake. Many, but certainly not all of them, were Nazis. A goodly number of businessmen found that their competitors were suddenly driven out of business and reacted with open or secret satisfaction. Others were rapidly promoted because executives were fired right and left for political or racial reasons. Minor playwrights and actors sometimes found never-dreamed-of opportunities. Not all these people were necessarily evil; it was made easy for them to give in to temptation. A great number of persons came forward and claimed that they had long been secret partisans of the Führer. It was not too difficult for them to supply some sort of proof. Besides, there were plenty of cautious individuals who wore the ribbon of Schuschnigg's Fatherland Front in their buttonholes and secretly paid dues to the illegal Nazi Party. Often this kind of prudence turned out to be very gainful. Others managed to join up at the very last moment when it became obvious that the Austrian government was in a state of collapse. With help from an understanding party secretary, membership cards were sometimes predated. In 1945, such worthies were frantic to make such embarrassing documents disappear. People who had joined the NSDAP out of sheer opportunism became known as "bread Nazis" or "March casualties."[1] They simply followed the slogan of the old English song: *"Whatever King shall reign,/ I will be the Vicar of Bray, Sir!"* The Nazi leadership was not worried about this rather doubtful type of support. People in government service or dependent on government orders were frequently pressured to join the party, which did not intend to become an elite of truly convinced supporters. Selectiveness could wait until the further development of the Thousand-Year Reich. In fact, the old "illegal" Nazis who had often fought for their ideals under considerable sacrifices found the easy acceptance of the latecomers rather shocking. The career of old party members during the following years proved sometimes disappointing. There was a definite tendency to place them in jobs outside of Austria.

The large number of carpetbaggers and profiteers swelled the ranks of the Nazis. From now on their fate was tied to the fortunes of the Third Reich. Its destruction would deprive them of their newly acquired property and their positions; therefore, they supported the regime for a long time until every hope for final victory was gone. The powerful propaganda of the National Socialist government was another important factor in shaping public opinion. Its initial impact in Austria was very strong. The average person had no recourse to foreign newspapers or magazines. Strict censorship made correspondence with foreign countries difficult. Travel abroad was restricted. Facts that contradicted the claims of the Nazi propaganda were carefully suppressed.

A political system that relies on deception and distortion cannot countenance the free expression of opinion. We have already mentioned that any form of criticism directed against the government was judged to be a serious crime. A law of that sort was bound to bring back the excesses of the most despotic Roman emperor.

[1] The expression "March casualties" originally referred to the revolution of 1848. They were persons killed during a riot.

Certain aspects of the police state had already existed under the old Hapsburg monarchy. During the long rule of Metternich,[2] a system of police informers was developed. The informer is an almost classical figure in Austrian literature, often in the comical disguise of a servant. Under the authoritarian regime of Dollfuss and Schuschnigg, police spies made their reappearance. Under Adolf Hitler they were omnipresent. The Gestapo preferred persons whose profession made it relatively easy to watch and to listen, like waiters and concierges. It became patriotic to denounce neighbors who made incautious remarks or lacked the proper enthusiasm for the Führer. This gave malicious or vindictive people a deadly weapon against anybody who aroused their antipathy. Resentful employees informed against their bosses and businessmen against their competitors. Disappointed girls denounced their previous lovers. Any old grudge could now be turned into a poisonous arrow. Five years of an anti-Nazi regime had left many resentments and grievances. But few people had expected the revenge that a suddenly all-powerful underworld would vent on its victims. The atmosphere of vigilantism and suspicion also spread to the schools, where the students were sometimes encouraged by fanatical Nazis to spy on their own parents. Denunciation did not always lead to prompt arrest. In doubtful cases the Gestapo merely registered the accusation but classified the persons in question as "politically unreliable." Later on, lists of such individuals were prepared; they were to be arrested in case of political unrest. In larger apartment buildings a *Blockwart* (block guardian) acted as watchdog and informer.

Every reign of terror brings the best and the worst elements of a nation to light. It produces martyrs and heroes, cowards and traitors, freedom fighters and informers. Invariably, the latent sadists, normally submerged, become its most ardent supporters and emerge as

---

[2] Klemens Wenzel Lothar von Metternich (1773–1859) was the leading Austrian statesman of the nineteenth century. From 1809 to 1848 his conservative policy was the foundation of the Hapsburg monarchy's position in Europe.

camp commanders or prison guards. The local bully boy turns into hangman or torturer. The history of dictatorship abounds in such individuals. On the other hand, unobtrusive persons sometimes show amazing courage and endurance. The brave ones always form a minority.

The situation in Austria differed from that of other European countries that were later occupied by the Germans. In the first place, it took the Nazis a comparatively short time to establish themselves. There was no language problem, and German officials could be placed in responsible positions without encountering too much difficulty. When World War II began, the key posts were safely in the hands of men who would not question any orders they received from Berlin. Secondly, young Austrians were immediately drafted into the German armed forces, thus the potential resistance lost the most important cadres. In Belgium, Holland, and Norway the young men of military age presented the most valuable reservoir for the fight for liberation. Worst of all, the Austrian draftees were mingled with Germans, and this made the formation of cohesive resistance groups almost impossible. The young Austrian who opposed Hitler found himself in well-disciplined German units, carefully watched by noncommissioned officers who regarded him with suspicion.

The great silent group of Austrians who did not welcome the *Anschluss* formed at first a hapless, intimidated mass of very heterogeneous citizens. They were leaderless, because all politicians of the First Republic were either imprisoned or in exile. Those who remained at liberty were forced to live in obscurity and silence. Schuschnigg's Fatherland Front had completely disintegrated and never was revived. The old political parties were in disarray. There was no help from abroad; even those who wanted to emigrate were not exactly welcomed with open arms. Political refugees were not very popular in the Western democracies. The world seemed to have written off Austria.

Lack of leadership was a problem that was to plague the Austrian opposition until the eventual liberation. At the time there was not even a clear alternative to permanent integration into the Reich. During the last years of the Republic, the possibility of a Hapsburg restoration had often been debated. Schuschnigg, a monarchist at heart, had pondered but finally rejected the idea out of fear of antagonizing not only Germany but also Yugoslavia and Czechoslovakia, whose old enmity against the Hapsburgs was still to be reckoned with. Archduke Otto,[3] a resident of Belgium, had a certain support, mainly among the older generation. However, no major power was willing to sustain a restored Austrian monarchy, and Otto himself was soon to appear as a refugee in the United States.

Only 17 months elapsed from the occupation of Austria until the invasion of Poland, which triggered World War II. In the meantime Czechoslovakia too had been absorbed into the Reich. Hitler's military power had increased, and to everybody's surprise Joseph Stalin concluded a nonaggression pact with the German dictator. No wonder Hitler's opponents in Austria felt isolated and depressed. With the outbreak of war they could take some faint hope that their oppressor would be eventually defeated. However, more than three years were to pass before the Germans suffered their first decisive setbacks.

Given this background, we should not find it surprising that the early resistance groups remained small and isolated. They consisted mainly of young people who were disgusted with the Nazi regime but had neither a clear-cut program nor any hope of speedy success. It took a great deal of youthful optimism to oppose Hitler in those dark days. They were like mice who conspired not against a cat, but against a jaguar. Well-meaning friends and relatives considered them impractical idealists, if not total fools. The risks of joining an underground group were terrifying. Capture by the Gestapo meant torture and long imprisonment in a concentration camp, often death. Even if a prisoner was released, he might well return with

---

[3] Born in 1912, he was the oldest son of the last Hapsburg emperor, Charles I, who had abdicated in 1918 and died in exile less than four years later, at age 35.

his health permanently ruined. Soon enough it became known that the mortality at the camps was very high. The next of kin were always informed when a prisoner died. This was done with the intention of striking terror into the hearts of potential opponents. Fear was the regime's most powerful psychological weapon. The truth about the horrible conditions in the camps spread only slowly, but no one had any illusions with regard to the treatment of the inmates.

For the German secret police, now permanently settled in the former Hotel Metropol, the relatively calm period prior to the outbreak of the war provided ample time to study conditions in Austria. As already mentioned, they had complete lists of all persons suspected of Leftist activities. The illegal Socialist party was now in the horrible situation of an "obsolete, defunct battle-ship, surrounded and exposed to mortal attacks from all sides," as a sympathetic historian[4] put it. The old party organization had to be completely disbanded. One larger illegal group, the Austrian Revolutionary Socialists (RSO), survived under extreme difficulties. They had already been active during the four years preceding the *Anschluss* and possessed a certain degree of experience in opposing an authoritarian government. However, the risks involved had now increased enormously. The illegal groups were constantly reduced by arrests and soon also by the compulsory transfer of workers to the Reich and by military draft calls. Carefully prepared operations frequently had to be abandoned because the participants were drafted into the armed forces.

The small Communist Party already had been banned by Doll-fuss in 1933. It possessed a well-organized underground network of dedicated members. Due to its small size it was better prepared for resistance work than larger, less versatile organizations that lacked trained leadership. Its conspiratorial character gave it a certain advantage. During the initial phase of the German occupa-tion, the Communist Party was intentionally kept small and it

[4] Joseph Buttinger, *Am Beispiel Österreichs* (Cologne: Verlag f. Politik u. Wirtschaft, 1953).

eliminated supporters of doubtful loyalty. Its propaganda division, the so-called "Lit Apparatus," was completely separated from all other party activities.

Hitler's unexpected nonaggression pact with Stalin (August 23, 1939) did not interrupt the relentless persecution of the Communists. The latter remained completely loyal to the Soviet Union, and a mocking rhyme was often heard in Vienna during those days:

> Behold our German Michel.[5]
> He now needs hammer and sickle.

His brief honeymoon with Stalin (August 23, 1939, to June 22, 1941) had no effect on Hitler's internal policy. He was well aware of the fact that the Communists remained dangerous opponents. The Gestapo and the German courts treated them with studied brutality. In December 1939 the whole Lit group, among it many women, was caught. In spite of this disaster it was soon rebuilt and it maintained its foremost illegal newssheet, "The Red Flag."

The conservative opposition against the National Socialists possessed at least one great unifying organization, the Roman Catholic Church. At first it had been hoped that Hitler would treat the Church with a degree of respect and consideration. This illusion was of very short duration. Cardinal Theodor Innitzer, who had obsequiously welcomed the *Anschluss*, soon had to learn the truth about Austria's new masters. In October 1938 the Roman Catholic Youth Organization staged a major demonstration in Vienna. The participants carried banners with the slogan "Jesus Christ is our leader," a clear rejection of National Socialism. Within a matter of hours the Nazis made a violent reply. The Hitler Youth attacked the Archbishop's Palace, insulted Innitzer, desecrated an altar, and destroyed many books and paintings. One priest was seriously injured. This event marked the first encounter between two ideologies which clearly were incompatible.

Innitzer was a well-meaning but timid man. Unlike several

---

[5] *"Der deutsche Michel"* personifies the German nation as John Bull does the British or Uncle Sam the US.

princes of the Church in Germany[6] and Holland,[7] he never exercised real leadership. But in smaller towns and villages the opposition against the Nazis was often led by the parish priest. The government's anti-Catholic attitude was bound to raise conflicts concerning schools, church meetings, holidays, and contributions. The abyss that separated the practicing Catholic from the National Socialist with his racial theory and new paganism could not be bridged. Six highly principled Catholics, one of them a priest, refused steadfastly to join the German army and were executed. Although the Church never openly endorsed resistance, a specifically Catholic opposition began to take form. The Church remained at least a spiritual force in Austria and presented a bulwark against the Nazi ideology.

The slowly growing resentment towards the occupying power on the part of the Austrian population can be studied from official German police records. There are increasing complaints about critical and unfriendly comments. At first there is only a negative attitude toward Germans in general, but soon the illegal pamphlet makes its appearance with texts such as "Prussian bloodsuckers, get out!" The Germans themselves admit that officials from the Reich "do not always act with tact toward the population." This was certainly an understatment. Occasionally, the pent-up anger of the Austrians led to minor demonstrations. During the performance of a classical play[8] the line "Law and justice must reign in German lands" was greeted with spontaneous applause. The public cheered those words night after night, but in this case the police showed a certain tolerance and allowed the performances to continue. Theater crowds were not judged to present a serious danger. In the same spirit the Viennese cabarets, long famous for

---

[6] Cardinal Michael Faulhaber, the bishops Preysing, Wiencken, Berning, and von Galen.

[7] Archbishop J. de Jong of Utrecht repeatedly condemned National Socialism. The Catholic Church in the Netherlands refused the sacraments to the Dutch Nazis.

[8] *König Ottokars Glück und Ende* (King Ottokar, his rise and fall) by Franz Grillparzer, a beloved Austrian classic.

their tongue-in-cheek satires, were allowed to perform in their old tradition. Companies such as the *Wiener Werkl* went on with thinly disguised attacks to the delight of their audiences. Not until September 1943 were all these smaller theaters closed.

4
THE FATE OF
THE EARLY UNDERGROUND

Some of the first serious acts of resistance occurred within the German armed forces. On March 13, 1939, just one year after the *Anschluss*, a 20-year-old soldier named Otto Vogl, born in Vienna, was sentenced to death and executed. Vogl belonged to a secret group which had its cells in several army barracks. When his organization was discovered, he escaped by taxi but was arrested at the Czech border after a brief exchange of shots. He became the first Austrian to be executed while serving in the German *Wehrmacht*. During the next months 13 young Austrians suffered the same fate for refusing to take an oath of loyalty to Adolf Hitler. One man, Franz Jägerstätter, a farmer from Upper Austria, deserves mention because of the remarkable notes he wrote while in prison awaiting execution.[1] His most touching memory is a letter written only a few hours before he faced the firing squad

---

[1] They inspired the American sociologist Gordon C. Zahn to write *In Solitary Witness: The Life and Death of Franz Jägerstätter* (New York: Holt, Rinehart & Winston, 1964).

in 1943. It does not contain one word of bitterness, only regret that his firm attitude brought sorrow to his family. This simple man, who also served as a sexton, is one of the many soft-spoken heroes of World War II.

With the outbreak of the war, life in Austria underwent a change. During the prewar period the economic situation had improved because the unemployed were absorbed by the expanding armament industry. But now the war-oriented economy began to affect the workers in many ways that no one had foreseen in 1938. The harsh facts of life under Hitler soon became apparent. Prices and taxes rose while wages remained unchanged. Workers were forcibly removed from their hometowns. It was forbidden to change jobs without a permit, and the work week was extended to 60 hours. The social rights which had been won by labor in the course of many decades by patient negotiation began to disappear at an alarming rate. The *Deutsche Arbeitsfront* (German Labor Front), which had replaced the labor unions, turned out to be mainly a propaganda machine that constantly pressured the workers for various contributions. In stark contrast, some of the Nazi leaders lived on a most extravagant scale.

The first serious unrest arose as a reaction to higher taxes and the compulsory transfer of Austrian labor to factories in the Reich. Workers were frequently shipped to German armament plants and given the worst jobs. In 1940 the authorities reported repeated protests as a result. The following example is typical: A Berlin ammunition plant applied to a labor exchange office in Austria for 400 female workers. However, only 80 reported for work, and those had to be escorted to the train by the local police.

Soon it dawned on the workers that the burden of the German war effort would fall mainly on their shoulders. Gradually, resistance in the factories began to rise. National Socialist propaganda could not affect workers who had been trained for decades by well-organized labor unions. In spite of the danger of arrest, acts of sabotage and passive resistance multiplied. Cells that promoted illegal activities formed in many factories. Most of these groups had to be small of necessity. If one member was captured, there was always the imminent danger that he would betray others under torture. Operations by small groups were safer, but their effectiveness was limited.

One of the first consequences of the war was an elaborate food rationing program. At the start some types of foods, like canned fish and chocolate, were still unrationed, but in the further course of the war not only all foodstuffs but also shoes, textiles, fuel, and other goods were subject to controlled distribution. Food coupons became a necessity of life. A person without a ration card would starve unless he had enough money to buy food on the black market. To obtain a ration card, valid personal identification papers were necessary. As a result, a person without proper papers was in an extremely difficult position. It is easy to understand how this affected men or women who tried to go underground.

The rationing process itself worked fairly well until the end of 1944. The population of Austria obtained 2,700 calories per person during the first years of World War II, and the per capita consumption never fell below 1,600 calories. Unlike what happened in other European countries, there was no starvation. The ruthless plundering of other nations provided the Reich with sufficient foodstuffs and many raw materials. In this respect Austria, as an integrated part of the Reich, was comparatively well off. Furthermore, almost anything could be purchased on the black market, but at a price. Therefore, the Austrian opposition against Hitler was not motivated by want or poverty, but mainly by hatred against oppression. That opposition reached from the extreme Left to conservative and monarchist circles.

One of the first of the conservative groups was founded by a Catholic priest, Roman Karl Scholz of the old Augustinian monastery of Klosterneuburg near the capital. Originally, Scholz had sympathized with the National Socialists, but after attending the Nuremberg party rally in 1937 he completely changed his mind. When the Germans occupied Austria, Scholz became one of their most determined adversaries. As an excellent linguist, the young priest was in a good position to establish foreign contacts. He did so at first during visits to Britain; later he also communicated with anti-Nazi groups in France and Czechoslovakia. Gradually he built up a secret organization which called itself *Österreichische Freiheitsbewegung* (Austrian Freedom Movement), abbreviated ÖFB.

Scholz realized that the time was not ripe for open rebellion and that the members of his organization—mainly students—had first to undergo ideological training. Later on he began to distribute literature that opposed the Nazis and the war, which had been caused by Hitler's policies. In April 1940, Scholz was ready to merge his group with two others that had similar aims but had been founded independently. One was led by an attorney, Jakob Kastelic, a former supporter of Schuschnigg, who also maintained contacts with the Socialists. The second group was headed by Karl Lederer, a civil servant. Together the three groups numbered about 1,000 members.

Unfortunately, the ÖFB had been infiltrated by a traitor who betrayed it to the Gestapo. This man was an actor at the prestigious Burgtheater, Otto Hartmann. Before the German invasion he had served with the paramilitary Austrian *Frontmiliz*. After the *Anschluss* he became a Nazi and joined the ÖFB, with the firm intention of delivering its members into the clutches of the Gestapo. Father Scholz and his friends were totally unaware of Hartmann's treacherous activity. The secret police proceeded with extreme caution and placed one of its most thorough and unscrupulous agents, Johann Sanitzer, at the head of the investigation. Hartmann was encouraged to continue to work with the Resistance and spur its members on to more decisive actions.

At Hartmann's suggestion, a major act of sabotage was to be undertaken. It was to start with a raid on an ammunition dump in the Vienna Woods. The purloined bombs were then to be used to blow up the large gas tank at Leopoldau. When all was prepared for action, Hartmann informed Sanitzer and the net closed on the unsuspecting freedom fighters. Of the 1,000 members of the secret organization, 240, among them the three leaders, were captured. The others remained at liberty because Hartmann did not know their names and their imprisoned friends did not betray them. Nevertheless, the disaster was almost complete. The German authorities took their time in destroying their adversaries. The arrested men were at first transferred to a German prison and were only brought to trial in 1944 before the dreaded People's Court in Vienna. The tribunal sentenced 11 defendants to death, but only 9 were actually executed. All the other received long prison sentences, and 5 of them perished during their confinement.

By the time Father Scholz and four of his companions were beheaded in May 1944, the tide of war had turned and Hitler's defeat was already approaching. The condemned men died with great courage, perhaps sustained by the conviction that their cause would ultimately triumph. One of the surviving prisoners, Father Ignaz Kühmayer, later described his gruesome experiences in a touching book.[2] The restored Austrian Republic has honored the memory of those martyrs. Today a square at Klosterneuburg commemorates the name of Roman Karl Scholz, and apartment houses built by the city of Vienna were named in honor of Jakob Kastelic.

Otto Hartmann, the informer who had caused the execution of 9 persons and prison terms totaling 362 years for the other defendants, was himself tried after the liberation by an Austrian court. He received a life sentence but was granted amnesty after having served 12 years in jail. Sanitzer, who had tormented numerous prisoners at Gestapo headquarters, was later arrested by the Soviet authorities and served 10 years in a Russian prison camp.

Father Scholz and his group can be considered representative of the conservative, predominantly Catholic resistance in the early part of World War II. Typical for a freedom fighter of the Socialist camp was the fate of Otto Haas. He came from an extremely poor family. Both his father and his mother were active in the Social Democratic Party. Young Otto Haas became a teacher and received

[2] *Auferstehung* (Vienna: Dom, 1947).

his PhD shortly before the *Anschluss*. At that time he was already in contact with a Socialist organization in Czechoslovakia and was trained in the technique of secret information. After the occupation of Austria he started to build up an underground apparatus with the task of distributing anti-Nazi reports. In May 1939, Haas was drafted and served in the meteorological service of the Luftwaffe, but this did not in the least prevent him from continuing his underground activity. Together with two other teachers, Eduard Göth and Josef Sommerauer, he organized the dissemination of secret information to contacts in Tyrol and Bavaria. The secret reports were hidden in bookcovers, pillows, and hollow keys, often in the form of small photostats. By 1940 Haas was in contact with Paris. He was very much aware of the importance of the news media. "Perhaps the most important weapon of fascism in suppressing any opposition is its monopoly of the news services," he wrote in one of his articles. He realized that a reliable news distribution was absolutely essential for a successful underground movement. One of the important couriers was a woman, Josefine Brunner of Wörgl, Tyrol.

In spring 1942 the Gestapo captured several men in Salzburg who had been in contact with Haas and his associates. From then on the whole underground system he had built was destroyed step by step. Frau Brunner and her husband were caught on April 26, 1942, in Wörgl, and two months later Haas himself was arrested. Eventually, his mother and the teachers Göth and Sommerauer were imprisoned as well.

The investigation that was carried out at Gestapo headquarters in Vienna took almost a year and a half. Haas was tortured for days in the so-called Chamber of Mirrors where the prisoners were constantly exposed to strong light beams reflected by mirrors. The trial against Haas, Göth, and Sommerauer was held in Berlin before the People's Court, presided over by judge Roland Freisler, who was notorious for his cruelty. By then Josefine Brunner and her husband had already been separately tried and executed.

The prosecutor called Haas "head of the revolutionary Socialists in the Greater German Reich" and asked for the death penalty. The court sentenced him and his friend Göth to die. Sommerauer received a 12-year prison sentence. Philomena Haas, Otto's mother, as well as several other implicated persons were tried in Vienna and drew various prison terms. Frau Haas survived and was elected to the Vienna City Council after the liberation of Austria.

As in the Scholz case, the authorities were in no hurry to carry out the death sentence. During several months Otto Haas and Father Scholz did indeed share the same prison cell. Haas spent his last days in the death cell of the Vienna district jail, his hands and legs chained. Finally, on August 30, 1944, Haas and 17 other prisoners were beheaded. According to the Protestant prison chaplain, Haas remained composed and full of courage to the very end. Each of the condemned men was led before the tribunal for identification and then promptly taken to a black curtain which led into the execution chamber. The delinquent was placed on a moveable stretcher that rolled beneath the automatic guillotine with its 110-pound blade. That ghastly procedure was so efficiently organized that only 4 to 8 minutes passed between the individual executions. The bodies were placed into caskets and shipped to the Anatomical Institute.

In all, more than 200 persons who belonged to Haas' underground organization were arrested, many of them in Bavaria. Of that total, 24 perished either by execution, suicide, or ill-treatment. The apartment building where Otto Haas lived today bears a memorial plaque with the following inscription:

> DR. OTTO HAAS
> FIGHTER FOR FREEDOM
> 1906–1944.

The fate of the ÖFB, the Haas group, and the Communist Lit organization is characteristic of the misfortunes that befell the early Austrian underground. There were many other small groups which suffered a similar fate. They were composed of dedicated men and women, but they lacked coordination and experience. Consequently, their effectiveness was small; they simply were not equipped for the deadly struggle with a well-organized and totally ruthless adversary. Furthermore, the Austrian Resistance during the first phase of the war had little contact with the Allies, who were themselves only gradually learning the technique of aiding and supplying the continental Resistance.

5
THE FINAL SOLUTION IN AUSTRIA

Since Adolf Hitler's rise to power on January 30, 1933, the German Jews had been subject to a growing number of discriminatory laws and regulations. The basic plan of the Nazis in those days was to force the Jews to leave Germany. However, this was a relatively slow and orderly process. Many older persons still hoped to be able to remain in their homeland to live out their days under restricted but still bearable conditions. By the time Austria was occupied, about half of the Jewish population had left the Reich.

With the integration of Austria, the technique of the Nazis changed. There were about 185,000 Jews in Austria, and it was decided to use the utmost pressure to force them to a hasty emigration. To achieve this, the Jews were not only made subject to all German racial laws and restrictions, but simultaneously were exposed to the most brutal terror. Immediately after the *Anschluss* a large number of Jews, mainly the wealthy and prominent citizens, were arrested. Many of them were later released, with strict orders to leave the country as soon as possible. Others simply disappeared into German concentration camps and never regained their freedom. In May 1938, about 2,000 Viennese Jews were suddenly arrested and shipped to the Dachau concentration camp. On November 10 the government organized an action against the Jews all over the Reich which was motivated by the assassination of a German embassy official in Paris. That day became known as *Kristallnacht* (Crystal Night or Night of Broken Glass), because the shopwindows of all Jewish stores were broken. Most synagogues were burned down; in many cases the homes of Jews were also ransacked. In Austria 4,600 Jews were arrested and sent to Dachau.[1]

Release was granted only if the prisoner could prove that all his documents for prompt emigration were ready. A few days after the outbreak of World War II, more than 1,000 stateless Jews, many of them inmates of old-age homes, were suddenly arrested and packed into cattle cars. They were shipped to the Buchenwald concentration camp and were so badly treated that by the summer of 1940 two-thirds of them had died. The older people in particular had little chance to survive the rigid conditions of the camp.

Those who remained at liberty—a precarious and very limited freedom—crowded the consulates and embassies of all foreign nations in a desperate effort to escape from a situation that became more critical from day to day. To obtain the necessary visa was by no means easy. Economic conditions in most countries were far from rosy, and as most refugees were now penniless there was little inclination to receive them. The Central Office for Jewish Emigration, established by the notorious Adolf Eichmann, completely stripped the emigrants of their property before they were allowed to leave the country. Nevertheless, about 56% of the Austrian Jews managed to emigrate prior to Hitler's attack on Poland.[2]

The speedy occupation of Poland gave the Nazis the opportunity

[1] Originally the number of arrested Jews was 7,800, but many were released.

[2] Great Britain admitted about 31,000 Austrian refugees, the United States approximately 29,000 and China about 18,000. About 9,000 went to Palestine and about 12,000 to Latin America. Altogether 128,000 Jews left Austria in the period from March 12, 1938, to November 1941.

to transport their victims to remote and unhealthy areas. In October 1939, two large groups of Jewish men, together about 1,500 persons, left Vienna for the area south of Lublin. The local Nazi governor recommended it as a Jewish reservation—"because of its very swampy nature," which would help in decimating the inhabitants. However, only about 200 of the deportees were put to work in the area and later returned to Vienna. The others were driven by the SS across the nearby Soviet border. The Russian authorities admitted the Jews but launched protests with the Germans, and the action was not repeated. The Jews who had entered Russia were left unmolested for a time, but eventually most of them were sent to labor camps in Siberia. For the Jews in Austria this isolated event was a sinister portent of things to come.

No further deportations took place until February 1941, but in the meantime the conditions for the Jews in Austria had greatly deteriorated. They were pressed into a ghetto, the old Jewish quarter of Vienna near the Danube Canal. They were forbidden to use public transportation, and most of them were now unemployed except those who were used as forced labor. Purchase of food was only permitted at certain hours, and from September 1941 on they had to wear a yellow star on their clothing. With the fall of France, Belgium, and Holland and the severe restrictions for overseas travel, emigration became almost impossible, and only a small number succeeded in leaving the country in 1940 and 1941. In November 1941, shortly before Pearl Harbor, emigration came to a complete halt. By then there were still 57,000 Jews in Austria, but they were now in a death trap.

The deportations had been resumed in February 1941. The Nazis followed a tactic which they also used in other occupied countries: the Jewish community itself was ordered to organize its own deportation. During 1941 about 10,000 Jews were shipped by train to various Polish towns and villages, where their arrival aggravated the already critical food situation. The Nazi governor of Poland, Hans Frank, repeatedly declared quite openly that he was not interested in feeding Jews.

Hitler had on various occasions threatened that European Jewry would eventually be destroyed. What became known as the "Final Solution of the Jewish Question" had been planned for a long time. In July 1941 Hermann Göring issued an order to the police and SD[3] chief Reinhard Heydrich in which all organizational measures for the mass killings were made the responsibility of Heydrich. Heydrich then directed Eichmann, his expert for Jewish affairs, to prepare the deportation of all Jews from Germany, Austria, and Czechoslovakia. All this more or less coincided with orders that were given at the start of the Russian campaign. Special police contingents (*Einsatzgruppen*) were formed, whose task consisted in rounding up and executing "all political commissars, all Jews, and all Communists." That order was valid for the occupied territories in the Soviet Union. For Heydrich this meant that Jews who were transported to that area automatically would be killed.

For the Jews who were still in the "Danube and Alpine districts"—the new Nazi nomenclature for Austria—these orders spelled their final doom. On October 15, 1941, the first transport of about 1,000 Jews left for Litzmannstadt (Lodz). During the next two weeks 4 similar transports followed. Some of these people died in the ghetto of Lodz from undetermined causes, but the majority were sent to a camp called Chelmno where they were killed by exhaust gases in sealed trucks.

Mass executions by firing squad had proved cumbersome, so more efficient methods for mass murder were created. The killings by means of exhaust gases were only a beginning. Soon this kind of gas was replaced by the faster-working hydrocyanic acid which was manufactured under the name of Zyklon B by IG Farben contractors. By this method large batches of people could be quickly and safely killed. The Germans developed this process into a sort of industry after having used it first in Hartheim, Austria, for killing mental patients.

---

[3] The SD (*Sicherheitsdienst*), originally the intelligence unit of the secret police, gradually became Hitler's secret service in all of German-controlled Europe.

On January 20, 1942, Heydrich held a conference of party and police leaders at the Wannsee, a lake near Berlin, and explained his program of dealing with the Jews in all parts of Europe controlled by the Reich. The Jews were at first to be interned in ghettos or transit camps and then transported to special death camps in Poland, where a selection was to take place. Those unsuited for hard labor were to be promptly gassed; the rest were to be put to work, but under conditions that would cause a "natural reduction." Those who became too weak or too ill to work were again to be eliminated, so that eventually all camp inmates would be destroyed. To achieve this, new camps were needed where that method could be practiced without attracting too much attention. The first district chosen for this so-called "Action Reinhard" was the area of Lublin, where a number of properly equipped camps were built. Odilo Globocnik, who for a short time had been district leader of Vienna, was appointed to head the operation. Two months later, Propaganda Minister Josef Goebbels noted in his diary: ". . . The Jews are now being moved eastward. A rather barbaric process, not to be described in detail, is being used. Not many Jews survive. About 60% have to be liquidated, only 40% can be used for labor. The former district leader of Vienna [Globocnik] is charged with that operation. He carries it out with adequate circumspection and in a not too conspicuous manner."

In Vienna the deportations continued during all of 1942, although the destinations varied. Several transports went to Riga, Latvia, where almost all of them, mostly old men, women, and children, were shot. A similar system was followed at Minsk. The deportees were taken right from the railroad station to previously prepared ditches and mowed down by the SS with automatic weapons. In April 1942, the destination changed again: the gas chambers in the Lublin district were now ready. Of the 6,000 Austrian Jews who were brought to that area, the majority was gassed in the death factories of Belzec and Sobibor.

By June 1942 the number of Jews in Vienna had been reduced to about 22,000. The Nazis now decided to divide them into two groups. About 8,000 were allowed to stay in Vienna. Most of these were married to gentiles; others worked for the *Kultusgemeinde* (Jewish Community Council), later replaced by the Council of Jewish Elders, or did forced labor. The rest—about 14,000 persons —were successively transferred to Theresienstadt (Terezin) in Bohemia, about 40 miles from Prague. It had been an old garrison town until Heydrich decided to make it a Jewish settlement for privileged Jews. The Czech population was evacuated. The first arrivals were Jews from Czechoslovakia, but later on Jews from Germany, Austria, and several occupied countries followed.

The Austrian Jews who were shipped to Theresienstadt were mainly older people who had so far been exempt from deportation: survivors of previous mixed marriage, veterans of World War I, persons of partly "Aryan" but predominantly Jewish ancestry,[4] employees of the Jewish Community Council, and a few prominent artists and scientists. Those people were told that at Theresienstadt they would live safely and peacefully under pleasant conditions.

Unfortunately the facts were different. By September 1942 the little town had been turned into a horribly overcrowded ghetto with 58,000 inhabitants living under the most unsanitary conditions. As more than half of that population was above 65, the mortality was frightfully high. Even the promised safety from further persecution proved to be an illusion. The town simply became another large transit camp, the last stop prior to extinction. Of the Austrian Jews who came to Theresienstadt, about 70% eventually ended up in the gas chambers of Auschwitz. The Jewish administration of Theresienstadt, which was headed during its last phase by a Viennese rabbi, Benjamin Murmelstein, could do nothing to prevent the deportations. The camp commander, Karl Rahm, also a Viennese, was executed as a war criminal after the liberation.

By the end of 1942 the Jewish population of Austria had shrunk

---

[4] See text of the Nuremberg laws. Persons with more than two Jewish grandparents were considered "full" Jews. Those with one or two Jewish grandparents were classified as "of mixed blood" (*Mischling*).

to about 8,000 persons, most of them married to gentiles. Before the end of the war their number was further diminished by about 1,600, most of whom were sent to Theresienstadt. Of the total of 67,600 deported Austrian Jews, only 2,142 returned after the war. Included in the 67,600 deportees were about 15,000 Austrian refugees who had emigrated to European countries that later fell under German domination. They were again arrested and deported when the extermination policy of the Nazis was applied to the occupied territories. There were only a few survivors who joined the underground in France and Holland.

In Austria itself only 219 Jews survived in hiding. This figure is very small, especially when compared with the number of "illegal" survivors in other occupied countries. In Denmark, for example, the major part of the Jewish population was saved by being transported clandestinely to Sweden. In the Netherlands about 8,000 Jews, half of them children, were successfully hidden from the Gestapo, and another 2,000 managed to escape to other countries. Why were so few Jews saved in Austria?

Undoubtedly, a family who would hide a Jew in their home took a tremendous risk. If found out, such people could only expect the most cruel treatment at the hands of the Gestapo and were certain to end up in a concentration camp. Furthermore, the fugitive had to be provided with forged papers and ration cards. Worst of all, if the person in hiding was easily recognizable as Jewish, he or she could never risk leaving his or her shelter. Such a person had to stay indoors for years, and even then there was always the danger of being observed by neighbors, by the concierge, or an unexpected visitor. This was less critical in countries where the majority of the population was hostile to the Germans and despised informers. In spite of this, many Jews in France and Holland were caught by the police due to malicious or gossipy neighbors. In Austria the Nazi system of block supervision was well organized, especially in Vienna, where the majority of the inhabitants lived in apartment houses that were easy to control.

Was the average Austrian aware of the atrocities that were

committed against the Jews? The newspapers claimed that the Jews were transferred to work camps so that they could make a contribution to the German war effort. The fact that the aged, the sick, and little children were also deported must have made this explanation sound very unconvincing. What useful labor could they perform? Among the Nazi party hierarchy the "Final Solution" was frequently discussed. Besides, the number of participants in the extermination policy was fairly large. Not all these people were actually executioners. Many were employed in offices that dealt with transportation, distribution of the victims' property, and similar matters. They certainly were aware of the true nature of those operations. Furthermore, those who worked in the area where the death camps were situated must have had a fairly precise idea of what went on in those installations. Last but not least, the Allies were well informed about the mass killings in Poland and Russia, and the BBC broadcast reports about the exterminations as early as the winter 1941/1942 in all languages. There is no doubt that these broadcasts were heard in Austria. Many listeners may have distrusted those stories and dismissed them as sheer enemy propaganda. Unfortunately, the reports were entirely correct.

Perhaps more Jews would have been saved if the deportations had not occurred at a time when most people still believed in a German victory. From the German police records it becomes quite clear that there were many Austrians who did not approve of the persecution of the Jews. But even the slightest gesture of sympathy was immediately punished. One man was arrested because he angrily tore up the anti-Semitic sheet *Der Stürmer*. A woman who had hidden jewelry and clothes that belonged to Jews was imprisoned and had her store confiscated. A number of people went to jail because they assisted Jewish friends in escaping across the border.

Most of the persons who were brave enough to shelter Jews against being deported were eventually caught, together with their lodgers. The following case illustrates the danger of such attempts. A Viennese family by the name of Kuttelwascher offered protection to a Jewish girl who had been designated for deportation to Poland. One day their neighbors noticed the girl's presence and warned Frau Kuttelwascher: "Send her away! Think of your own children. This will end very badly!" However, later on the neighbor's wife changed her mind. "Let her stay. Today I saw Jews being transported. I cannot be responsible for such a fate." The girl remained hidden in her hosts' apartment and survived the war.

Some of the most spectacular actions to save Jews were undertaken by Austrian soldiers who served in the German *Wehrmacht.* Perhaps the most impressive case is that of the Viennese Sergeant Anton Schmid, 47 years old, a man of truly heroic mold. Schmid was in charge of an army post near Vilna, Lithuania. In this capacity he employed a large number of Jewish laborers. He managed to help many of those Jews to escape from the Vilna ghetto. Some of them succeeded in reaching the port of Libau and eventual safety in Sweden. In November 1941 Schmid came in contact with the Jewish underground and organized a transport of 300 Jews from the ghetto to Bialystok. In April 1942 the German police discovered Schmid's activities. He was arrested, court-martialed, and immediately executed. Before facing the firing squad, he wrote his wife and daughter as follows: ". . . Please forgive me. I have only acted as a human being and did not wish to hurt anyone." The State of Israel later honored Schmid's memory. Another brave man was Ewald Kleisinger, who served as an officer in Warsaw while the battle in the Jewish ghetto was raging. He helped to save three Jewish escapees, hid them in his own room, and finally sent them with forged papers to his parents in Vienna, where they survived.

The great majority of the population, however, did not rise to such heroic behavior. They were either too indifferent or too scared to act with defiance. Even the churches were extremely cautious in their approach, and only a limited number of priests dared to take a firm stand. The case of Alexander Seewald, parish priest of Mürzsteg, clearly illustrates the danger of such an attitude. During his Christmas sermon in 1939, Father Seewald emphasized that

Jesus was a Jew and "consequently the descent of a human being can never be a crime." Two weeks later the priest was arrested and had to spend the next five years in a concentration camp.

The churches had the additional problem of the converted Jews who according to Hitler's racial politics were in no way exempt from persecution. Cardinal Innitzer, who found the policies of Hitler less and less to his liking, tried to save at least the Catholics who were of Jewish extraction. His main effort was directed towards assisting those persons with their emigration. His correspondence with Pope Pius XII and various foreign bishops makes very sad reading, for he could obtain only little aid and had to haggle about paltry sums of money. Eventually, he managed to make the emigration of 150 Catholic converts possible.

Several Protestant organizations, for example, the Society of Friends and a committee founded by the Dutch Reverend C. H. Gildemeester, also tried to help Jews. Their activities came to an end in 1941.

Persons with only two Jewish grandparents were not deported but were subject to many restrictions. There were about 26,000 such people in Austria. Discrimination began in school. Fanatical Nazi teachers relegated the "mixed" students to the back benches and prohibited the other students from talking to them.

The story of the Final Solution in Austria is certainly a gloomy one and has not ceased to trouble the conscience of Austrian writers and historians to this day. Even if it is true that the long economic crisis from 1929 to 1938 greatly contributed to Hitler's success, the question remains: Why was the Austrian soil so fertile for his particularly virulent brand of anti-Semitism? Perhaps a complete and impartial answer will be found only when the generation which took an active or a passive part in those events is gone.

rity in Austria. These Slavs had been inhabitants of
many centuries. After the collapse of the Yugoslavian
orderlands were incorporated into the Reich, and the
oth sides of the new frontier were treated very badly.
ee later, this borderland eventually became a foothold
activity.

ity toward the "Slavic subhumans" was growing. It
directed against the relatively large Czech minority.
functionaries openly declared that the Czechs were
irable and should be driven from German soil. Events
rakia inflamed the traditional hatred on both sides. In
941 the particularly bloodthirsty Reinhard Heydrich,
anizer of the "Final Solution," was appointed acting
overnor) of Bohemia and Moravia. Heydrich pro-
extreme brutality against the Czech intelligentsia. At
e he tried to neutralize workers and farmers by means
concessions. His reign came to an abrupt end when
olown up by two Czech paratroopers who had been
a an RAF plane. Heydrich's spine was shattered and he
ys after the attack. There followed an orgy of revenge.
Czechs were executed, and the village of Lidice was
he face of the earth after most of the inhabitants had
ed. The Germans of Czechoslovakia were to pay dearly
ery in 1945.

s found after the war make it clear that in case of a
ory the Czechs would have suffered a sinister fate.
vould prove adaptable were to be "Germanized," the
ed or destroyed. These plans were not to be discussed
ar, because unpleasant repercussions were expected.

tide began to turn against Germany, the Nazi authori-
scared and a secret memorandum warned against pro-
lavic nations. It was proclaimed that their cooperation
e. The order was given mainly to avoid unrest and to
ators. It remained futile and could not prevent serious
oland, Yugoslavia, and Slovakia. In the end Hitler's

6
THE INTERNAL SITUATION UP TO 1943

Shortly after the collapse of France, Josef Bürckel, *Reichsstatthalter* (governor) and district leader of Vienna, was transferred to Alsace-Lorraine. Hitler was aware of the fact that this man, his highest-ranking representative in Austria, had remained a total stranger in the country he was to integrate into the Reich. A new personality was needed, a man who would make the Nazi regime more palatable to the Austrians, especially to the Viennese, who lacked the proper enthusiasm for the new order.

The new overlord was presented to his subjects on August 10, 1940. His name was Baldur von Schirach; he was 33 years old and had been the leader of the Hitler Youth as well as a lieutenant in the *Wehrmacht*. Schirach was a somewhat unusual personality among the Nazi bigwigs. The son of an aristocratic German officer and an American lady of respectable family, he had joined the party as an 18-year-old student. He had the pretensions of an *homme de lettres*; in fact, he wrote third-rate poems that dealt with self-sacrifice and marble monuments. Handsome and of gentlemanly demeanor, Schirach opposed violence and cruelty when they became all too visible. The Führer expected that this man of romantic nature and literary affectations would captivate the Viennese.

Soon afterwards, the mayor of Vienna, a moderate Austrian Nazi by the name of Hermann Neubacher, was shifted to a diplomatic post in Romania. He was succeeded by a German official, Philipp Wilhelm Jung, who was a complete stranger to Vienna and remained isolated from the population during his three years in office. The deputy mayor (and Jung's successor), Hanns Blaschke, was a product of the Austrian SS with good connections to Berlin. This man had ambitions of his own and was extremely antagonistic to Schirach, who did his best to ignore him. The other district leaders—there were six of them—were mostly local Nazis who did not like Schirach. Intrigues to depose him increased from year to year but remained unsuccessful.

It must be remembered that in 1940 most people still believed in a German victory. France had been decisively defeated; Denmark, Norway, Holland, and Belgium were occupied territories. Poland had been divided between the Reich and the Soviet Union, and relations between the two great dictatorships still seemed cordial. Italy and Japan were Hitler's allies and the United States was still neutral. Only Britain was fighting, but since all operations took place at sea or in the air, the war seemed somewhat remote. In North Africa the Italians were opposing the British, whose desert victories were still in the future. Many citizens who were by no means sympathetic to Hitler believed that his chances for ultimate victory were excellent.

Of course, there had been casualties, especially among the alpine troops[1] who fought in Norway. These soldiers came mainly from the mountainous regions of Austria. However, until the beginning of the Russian campaign (June 22, 1941), losses were not excessive. Many families still led a comparatively normal life. All

[1] These Austrian alpine troops (*Gebirgsjäger*) later saw action in Greece, on Crete, and in the Caucasus. Most of them eventually perished in the Volkhov marshes in 1944.

weekend trains were crowded be combined pleasure with the chanc

Southeastern Europe became activity and intrigue. In July 194 Romanian provinces. A long-smo and Romania was solved by the conference on August 31, 1940, and Italy forced Romania to cede tries were now quickly becoming came under stronger German coming and going of Balkan di to become a new center of pol had been in the faraway days o von Schirach began to behave with the pretensions of a Balkan more luxurious than that of ar to the Ballhausplatz, previously ment, while his offices occupied The Hofburg, once the imperia rate receptions at which Schira in the most opulent style. At th plans which were to take for Schirach did not foresee that a be turned into rubble.

At first, the dream of don seemed to become reality. In A within 11 days, Greece was occ forces narrowly escaped disaste of Crete fell to the German p were aware of the fact that the the attack on Russia, already i four fateful weeks. The Gern short-lived; in 1941 the serio rugged country was not yet un

The occupation of Yugosl

Slove
Carin
army
Slove
As w
for g

Th
was
Some
racial
in Cze
Septer
the m
protec
ceeded
the sa
of eco
his car
droppe
expired
About
wiped
been m
for that

Docu
Germa
Those
others
during

Whe
ties bec
voking
was des
gain col
revolts

racial policy brought disaster to all Germans, good or bad, who for many centuries had lived peacefully among the Slavic nations.

The small Croatian minority in the eastern parts of Austria also aroused the suspicion of the Nazis. It was feared that the Croats had "Pan-Slavic" feelings and saw in Russia "their big Slavic brother." The German authorities tried to discourage this national group by drafting the leaders into the army and by arresting those who were considered anti-German.

The problem of the Slavs in Austria was accentuated by the arrival of Polish prisoners of war. The attitude of the Austrian population toward the Poles, who were used as laborers, was generally friendly. A number of police reports on that subject have survived; they are full of angry remarks about the sympathy shown to the Poles by the farmers, sometimes even by Austrian guards. With rage it is noted that the rustic population had no aversion to the Polish soldiers, who were "not considered enemies but fellow Catholics." In some cases the villagers collected clothing and money for the POWs, who on occasion had to march without shoes. A complete lack of decency and fairness toward the defeated enemy is evidenced by various reports in which the SD complains that Poles received wine and cigarettes from the local population and were allowed to attend church on Christmas eve. What enraged the Nazis most of all was the fact that Austrian girls sometimes entered into intimate relations with Polish prisoners. From 1940 on POWs who committed that "racial crime" were executed. The girls were shorn of their hair, pilloried, and shipped to the concentration camp of Ravensbrück, where they were repeatedly flogged. This camp for female prisoners had been built in 1939 and turned into an inferno where the inmates were not only used as forced labor but also for medical experiments by a team of German physicians. Sick or infirm prisoners were gassed or killed by injections; on one occasion about 700 were killed in a day. The female prison guards were often more cruel than the men, and sadistic tortures like burying women up to the neck or pouring ice cold water on them in freezing weather were not uncommon.

Some inmates who were appointed "capos" managed to save other prisoners. A young Czech girl from Vienna, Anni Vavak, whose task it was to lead a column of prisoners to their daily work, was a shining figure of humanity in this place of horror.

While the day of reckoning with the Slavic nations was postponed, no such caution was deemed necessary with regard to the Gypsies, another minority that was considered racially inferior by the Nazis. Prejudice against that wandering nation had always been widespread; demands for their expulsion had been made as early as 1933. The Nazis decided to solve the Gypsy problem once and for all. At first the Gypsies were confined to the Burgenland, the easternmost part of Austria, which borders on Hungary. Once concentrated in this area, they became an easy prey for the SD. In April 1940 deportations to Poland started. Eventually the Gypsies were brought to Auschwitz and other death camps, where most of them perished.

The terror against certain religious sects was increased. The persecution was mainly directed against the Seventh Day Adventists and the International Bible Students or Jehovah's Witnesses. These religious groups rejected military service and maintained close connections with their coreligionists abroad. In December 1940 Anton Strezak, a member of Jehovah's Witnesses, was executed as a conscientious objector—the first of a great number of victims in Austria. During the first year of World War II, 1,917 Jehovah's Witnesses were sentenced to death in the Reich. The charge was always the same: corrupting the *Wehrmacht.* A far greater number of these sectarians, men and women, were shipped to concentration camps. Their quiet courage often impressed the other inmates.

A peculiar situation developed in South Tyrol, a part of Austria that had been annexed by Italy in 1919. Though the population was predominantly German by language and ancestry, Hitler made no attempt to claim their territory, for he wished to avoid a conflict with Mussolini. Instead he accommodated his ally by a cynical treaty concerning a transfer of population that was concluded in

October 1939. The inhabitants could either opt for emigration to the Reich or become true Italians. Of the South Tyroleans, 58% voted for "return to the Reich," but only about 80,000—a third of the total population—actually were resettled.[2] In the fall of 1941 the whole action ground to a halt; the Italians, whose military situation was deteriorating, had more important worries. In the meantime, no one knew what to do with the new arrivals. The governor of the recently occupied Crimea, an Austrian Nazi with a fertile imagination, suggested that the South Tyroleans be shipped to that part of Russia. Fortunately for the people concerned, the Crimea was reconquered by the Russians before this adventurous plan could be carried out.

In spite of so many violent events, social life in Vienna went on at a brisk pace. Baldur von Schirach established himself as a great patron of art and music. He wished to make Vienna attractive for Balkan visitors and personally invited his guests to sample the city's night life. Prostitutes often were employed by the Gestapo as useful informers.

For the theater a new general manager (*Generalreferent*) was appointed, one Walter Thomas, another German in a key position. His background was not impressive, but Schirach did not want an Austrian in so sensitive a job. Thomas was a fairly decent person, who eliminated the infamous stool pigeon Hartmann from the Burgtheater and occasionally tried to help actors who were Jewish or who in some other way were considered undesirable. He immediately came into conflict with Deputy Mayor Blaschke, who was a fanatical SS man but hated Prussians.

In his eagerness to stimulate Vienna's cultural life, Schirach initiated festivals in memory of great Austrian poets and composers. In a ludicrous manner they were always presented as German folk heroes, although this was in contradiction to historical fact. Many Viennese must have been slightly astonished when, for example,

[2] These figures are somewhat doubtful. According to other sources, only 64,000 persons left South Tyrol.

Franz Grillparzer,[3] Austria's greatest poet, was described by Schirach as a Pan-German. It would have been easy to quote from his works and arrive at very different conclusions.[4] Naturally, some local authors, for example, the poet Josef Weinheber and the novelist Bruno Brehm, were happy to serve the regime. Others, less enthusiastic, easily bowed to pressure. They had the ready excuse that writers were bound to their native language and would starve abroad. There were also some noteworthy exceptions like the poetess Paula von Preradovic, who was later imprisoned but survived. Another talented writer, Alma Johanna König, who happened to be Jewish, was deported and perished at Minsk. Her last novel, published long after her death, dealt—almost prophetically—with the Emperor Nero. Two other Jewish authors, the poet Jura Soyfer and the lawyer and novelist Heinrich Steinitz, also perished.

The writers, composers, and artists who willingly became Hitler's lackeys could point to some prominent colleagues in the Reich who had indeed set them a very bad example. Gerhart Hauptmann, doyen of the German drama, had long since declared his loyalty to Hitler. His early work had been of a pronounced socialist tendency, but the Nazis were in need of converts with a reputation and all was forgiven. In 1942, Hauptmann celebrated his eightieth birthday in Vienna and was widely cheered. Undoubtedly, vanity, the fear of losing his royalties, and old age were equally responsible for the aged author's attitude.[5]

A similar case was that of Richard Strauss, then Germany's greatest and most versatile living composer. Strauss lived in Bavaria but moved to Vienna in 1941 at the invitation of Baldur von Schirach. An unlikely convert to National Socialism, Strauss had a Jewish daughter-in-law and had worked with Jews during his entire career. Perhaps his cooperation with the Nazis was at least

[3] Franz Grillparzer (1791–1872) was the author of several tragedies dealing with historical subjects.
[4] For example: "The Prussian art of acquisition is like thievery during a blaze." Or: "The path of modern culture leads from humanity via nationality to bestiality."
[5] Predictably, after the war Hauptmann welcomed the Russians. He died in 1946.

partly dictated by the wish to protect his family. In Vienna, Strauss was treated as an honored guest, lived on a grand scale, conducted the Philharmonic Orchestra, and received the Beethoven award. His daughter-in-law and her two children remained unmolested.

Vienna's theaters were extremely active during the first phase of the war. There was certainly no lack of an audience, for most people were very glad to forget the war for a few hours. In strange contrast, long lines formed every morning in front of the Viennese prisons. These were mostly women who wanted to bring food and clothes to their husbands, sons, or other relatives who were languishing in jail. And while Herr von Schirach was making his pompous speeches on German culture and its European mission, strange things were taking place at Hartheim Castle in Upper Austria. Transports of insane, incurably sick, or crippled patients arrived and never left. The victims were shipped in regular post buses and unloaded in the courtyard. Then they were told to undress and walk into the "bathroom." That room was equipped with gas pipes that emitted poison gas. Three adjoining ovens worked day and night to consume the bodies. The remnants were loaded into trucks and deposited in the river Danube. That was Hitler's euthanasia program, an efficient process to destroy "biologically inferior persons." Similar installations existed in Germany, sometimes directly connected with homes for the mentally sick.

Hartheim fell under the administration of the camp commandant of Mauthausen. This made it possible to send sick or disabled camp inmates to the Hartheim gas chamber. They were simply shipped to the castle "for special treatment." Altogether about 30,000 human beings were liquidated at Hartheim. The population of the surrounding villages was probably well aware of what was going on because of the ghastly odor which emanated from the ovens as well as the bones and ashes which often dropped from the trucks.

What is really amazing is the fact that during the five years the euthanasia program was functioning, no physician in Austria raised his voice to protest. There can be no doubt that numerous doctors fully realized that their patients were being killed. The disappearance of so many inmates of various medical and mental institutions cannot possibly have gone unnoticed. Furthermore, the extermination took place not in faraway Poland but only 17 miles from the city of Linz. One can only conclude that the doctors were either too scared to dissent or agreed with the systematic liquidation of the victims.

Baldur von Schirach, Hitler's gentlemanly satrap in Austria, never showed the slightest inclination to mitigate the Nazi terror in Austria. Later, as a defendant at Nuremberg and in his memoirs, he disclaimed knowledge of the assorted horrors that were committed under his authority. His allegations do not deserve credence. A report of the German Department of Justice mentions that he was among those district leaders who never intervened for persons doomed to die. His colleagues in Salzburg and Lower Austria were not quite so merciless. It is interesting to note that Henriette von Schirach, the *Gauleiter's* lady, made a lone attempt to help the Jews during a visit to Hitler's retreat in Berchtesgaden. The Führer told her rudely to mind her own business. Her husband proudly took credit for the disappearance of the Jews at a Youth Congress in September 1942.

If Baldur von Schirach were ignorant regarding the fate of the deportees, he could easily have obtained information from an Austrian SS officer whom he frequently met at dinners and receptions. The name of this man was Ernst Kaltenbrunner. Until 1938 he had been a lawyer at Linz and an eager but not very well known supporter of the illegal Nazi Party. During the next years he rose in the ranks of the SS, but his name was rarely mentioned in the newspapers. A tall man of cold, aloof behavior, he was not one of the Nazi celebrities. Kaltenbrunner's hour came when Heydrich, chief of the SD, was assassinated in Prague. Kaltenbrunner became his successor, the only Austrian who rose to a high position in the Nazi government. In the last three years of the war he signed every order that referred to arrests, deportations, and special executions. During the period he was one of the most powerful men in German-controlled Europe. He must have been a worried police chief in November 1942, because during that month the whole situation underwent a decisive change.

Within two weeks Rommel's Afrika Korps was defeated at El Alamein, the Allies landed in North Africa, and the Sixth German Army was encircled by the Russians between the Volga and the Don. The German news reports made light of these setbacks, but the casualty lists mounted in an alarming way. The disasters of Tunis and Stalingrad were still to come, but confidence in a German victory began to wane.

7
STALINGRAD AND AFTER

On February 2, 1943, the last remnants of 22 German divisions that had been encircled at Stalingrad laid down their arms. This time it was not possible to hide the plain facts of the debacle. Among the 90,000 soldiers who surrendered to the Russians were many Austrians. According to rumors, all German POWs were shot, but the Austrians were treated well. This was of course pure invention. Actually, only a few thousand prisoners survived; the majority simply died from injuries, exhaustion, and epidemics.

The police reported alarming incidents in Austria. When told that his son had fallen, a farmer tore a Hitler photo from the wall and threw it at the Nazi official who had brought the bad news. A woman informed of her son's death slapped a Nazi functionary's face. A Swedish journalist who visited Austria in early 1943 wrote: "Five years of German nationalist domination have revived the Austrian idea. . . . The Austrians reject not only National Socialism but German nationalism itself. The capital of old Austria is lost to the Third Reich. . . . Even Graz, once a Nazi bulwark, has thoroughly changed."[1] Hatred of the "Prussians" was now hardly disguised; the expression "Prussian" or "Piefke" was widely applied to everybody who hailed from the Reich. Even party members sometimes showed their aversion to the "German brethren."

Stalingrad changed the face of the war. Until 1943 the German government hesitated to impose strict austerities on the nation, especially on the privileged classes. The British had lowered the level of private comfort far more drastically and also employed a greater number of women in their armament industries. In Germany many leading party members and officials lived in great luxury. Others found convenient shelters in the occupied territories, where the German rulers adopted the ways of the parasitic proconsuls of imperial Rome. The immensely complicated structure of the regime led to waste and disorganization. The Germans relied to a large extent on forced labor from the subject nations and subsequently on troops from allied or occupied countries. Those often unwilling soldiers and workers became a liability in the last years of the war. In Russia and in the Balkans the guerrilla war had grown to alarming dimensions. By the end of 1942 the Yugoslav partisan armies consisted of about 150,000 men, and minor actions began to affect the borderland of Carinthia.

The dictatorship felt threatened and the terror was intensified. All through 1942 there had been arrests of malcontents, dissidents, and actual resistance fighters. But like the mythical hydra, for every severed head the growing discontent sprouted new ones.

Propaganda Minister Josef Goebbels appointed a special observer, one Egon Arthur Schmidt, to attend the trials before the People's Court. His reports are revealing. In Graz alone, 64 persons were in the dock within two weeks and 43 of them drew death sentences. At one trial in Vienna the defendant was carried into the courtroom on a stretcher. He had cut his arteries on the day before the session. In another case, the trial of a Socialist func-

[1] Awil Fredborg, *Behind the Steel Wall* (London: Harrap, 1944).

tionary, 8 of the witnesses for the prosecution were already under sentence of death. Schmidt remarks that even the Nazis in the audience were impressed by their brave behavior. Of course, witnesses and accused were all executed.

Meanwhile, Ernst Kaltenbrunner, the new chief of the *Reichssicherheitsamt* or RSHA (Reich Security office) grew into his job. On several occasions he visited the concentration camp at Mauthausen and attended executions of male and female inmates. At the Vienna District Court the executioner Alois Weiss and his aides were busy men. In that building alone 1,200 persons were beheaded during the period of German occupation. The rising number of executions in the armed services is revealing as well. Daily life became more strenuous. Food rations were decreased and many small business enterprises had to close because of lack of raw materials. Church bells were confiscated as metal became scarce. A number of children from the bombed cities of the Reich were evacuated to Austria.

For the Nazi leisure class, life was still pleasant. Baldur von Schirach acquired an elegant private home in a Vienna suburb. The party functionary, Eduard Frauenfeld, not to be outdone, lived in sumptuous style in another manor that had been confiscated from a Jewish owner. Some of his colleagues complained to Berlin about such wastefulness, but to no avail. Schirach himself was now far from popular with the party leadership in Berlin. It was thought that he spent too much money for unnecessary congresses. He was also accused of meddling in foreign policy. Some of the art exhibitions that were sponsored by the Vienna district leader aroused the ire of Goebbels, who considered the paintings *"entartet,"* the work of degenerates.[2] However, no proper replacement for Schirach was found, and he kept his position to the bitter end. The cultural manager Thomas had to be sacrificed and was replaced by a Nazi nonentity.

In the meantime, the underground Resistance received some un-

[2] An exposition of "Young Art in the German Reich" was closed prematurely on orders from Berlin.

6
THE INTERNAL SITUATION
UP TO 1943

Shortly after the collapse of France, Josef Bürckel, *Reichsstatthalter* (governor) and district leader of Vienna, was transferred to Alsace-Lorraine. Hitler was aware of the fact that this man, his highest-ranking representative in Austria, had remained a total stranger in the country he was to integrate into the Reich. A new personality was needed, a man who would make the Nazi regime more palatable to the Austrians, especially to the Viennese, who lacked the proper enthusiasm for the new order.

The new overlord was presented to his subjects on August 10, 1940. His name was Baldur von Schirach; he was 33 years old and had been the leader of the Hitler Youth as well as a lieutenant in the *Wehrmacht*. Schirach was a somewhat unusual personality among the Nazi bigwigs. The son of an aristocratic German officer and an American lady of respectable family, he had joined the party as an 18-year-old student. He had the pretensions of an *homme de lettres*; in fact, he wrote third-rate poems that dealt with self-sacrifice and marble monuments. Handsome and of gentlemanly demeanor, Schirach opposed violence and cruelty when they became all too visible. The Führer expected that this man of romantic nature and literary affectations would captivate the Viennese.

Soon afterwards, the mayor of Vienna, a moderate Austrian Nazi by the name of Hermann Neubacher, was shifted to a diplomatic post in Romania. He was succeeded by a German official, Philipp Wilhelm Jung, who was a complete stranger to Vienna and remained isolated from the population during his three years in office. The deputy mayor (and Jung's successor), Hanns Blaschke, was a product of the Austrian SS with good connections to Berlin. This man had ambitions of his own and was extremely antagonistic to Schirach, who did his best to ignore him. The other district leaders—there were six of them—were mostly local Nazis who did not like Schirach. Intrigues to depose him increased from year to year but remained unsuccessful.

It must be remembered that in 1940 most people still believed in a German victory. France had been decisively defeated; Denmark, Norway, Holland, and Belgium were occupied territories. Poland had been divided between the Reich and the Soviet Union, and relations between the two great dictatorships still seemed cordial. Italy and Japan were Hitler's allies and the United States was still neutral. Only Britain was fighting, but since all operations took place at sea or in the air, the war seemed somewhat remote. In North Africa the Italians were opposing the British, whose desert victories were still in the future. Many citizens who were by no means sympathetic to Hitler believed that his chances for ultimate victory were excellent.

Of course, there had been casualties, especially among the alpine troops[1] who fought in Norway. These soldiers came mainly from the mountainous regions of Austria. However, until the beginning of the Russian campaign (June 22, 1941), losses were not excessive. Many families still led a comparatively normal life. All

[1] These Austrian alpine troops (*Gebirgsjäger*) later saw action in Greece, on Crete, and in the Caucasus. Most of them eventually perished in the Volkhov marshes in 1944.

weekend trains were crowded because excursions into the country combined pleasure with the chance to purchase food from the farms.

Southeastern Europe became the object of frantic political activity and intrigue. In July 1940, the Soviet Union occupied two Romanian provinces. A long-smoldering conflict between Hungary and Romania was solved by the so-called Vienna Award. At this conference on August 31, 1940, the foreign ministers of Germany and Italy forced Romania to cede territory to Hungary. Both countries were now quickly becoming satellites of the Axis, and Bulgaria came under stronger German influence. There was a constant coming and going of Balkan diplomats in Vienna, which seemed to become a new center of political and economic activity, as it had been in the faraway days of the Hapsburg monarchy. Baldur von Schirach began to behave like a sort of Nazi student prince with the pretensions of a Balkan ruler. His way of life was certainly more luxurious than that of any Hapsburg emperor. He moved to the Ballhausplatz, previously the seat of the Austrian government, while his offices occupied the former parliament building. The Hofburg, once the imperial palace, was used for overelaborate receptions at which Schirach's guests were wined and dined in the most opulent style. At the same time, fantastic architectural plans which were to take form after the war were announced. Schirach did not foresee that a good part of Vienna would by then be turned into rubble.

At first, the dream of dominance over southeastern Europe seemed to become reality. In April 1941 Yugoslavia was smashed within 11 days, Greece was occupied, and the British expeditionary forces narrowly escaped disaster by a hasty retreat. Even the island of Crete fell to the German paratroopers. Only very few persons were aware of the fact that the victorious Balkan campaign delayed the attack on Russia, already in a far-advanced planning state, for four fateful weeks. The German triumph in Yugoslavia proved short-lived; in 1941 the seriousness of partisan warfare in that rugged country was not yet understood.

The occupation of Yugoslavia had a serious impact on the

Slovene minority in Austria. These Slavs had been inhabitants of Carinthia for many centuries. After the collapse of the Yugoslavian army, some borderlands were incorporated into the Reich, and the Slovenes on both sides of the new frontier were treated very badly. As we shall see later, this borderland eventually became a foothold for guerrilla activity.

The hostility toward the "Slavic subhumans" was growing. It was mainly directed against the relatively large Czech minority. Some Nazi functionaries openly declared that the Czechs were racially undesirable and should be driven from German soil. Events in Czechoslovakia inflamed the traditional hatred on both sides. In September 1941 the particularly bloodthirsty Reinhard Heydrich, the main organizer of the "Final Solution," was appointed acting protector (governor) of Bohemia and Moravia. Heydrich proceeded with extreme brutality against the Czech intelligentsia. At the same time he tried to neutralize workers and farmers by means of economic concessions. His reign came to an abrupt end when his car was blown up by two Czech paratroopers who had been dropped from an RAF plane. Heydrich's spine was shattered and he expired six days after the attack. There followed an orgy of revenge. About 1,300 Czechs were executed, and the village of Lidice was wiped from the face of the earth after most of the inhabitants had been massacred. The Germans of Czechoslovakia were to pay dearly for that savagery in 1945.

Documents found after the war make it clear that in case of a German victory the Czechs would have suffered a sinister fate. Those who would prove adaptable were to be "Germanized," the others deported or destroyed. These plans were not to be discussed during the war, because unpleasant repercussions were expected.

When the tide began to turn against Germany, the Nazi authorities became scared and a secret memorandum warned against provoking the Slavic nations. It was proclaimed that their cooperation was desirable. The order was given mainly to avoid unrest and to gain collaborators. It remained futile and could not prevent serious revolts in Poland, Yugoslavia, and Slovakia. In the end Hitler's

racial policy brought disaster to all Germans, good or bad, who for many centuries had lived peacefully among the Slavic nations.

The small Croatian minority in the eastern parts of Austria also aroused the suspicion of the Nazis. It was feared that the Croats had "Pan-Slavic" feelings and saw in Russia "their big Slavic brother." The German authorities tried to discourage this national group by drafting the leaders into the army and by arresting those who were considered anti-German.

The problem of the Slavs in Austria was accentuated by the arrival of Polish prisoners of war. The attitude of the Austrian population toward the Poles, who were used as laborers, was generally friendly. A number of police reports on that subject have survived; they are full of angry remarks about the sympathy shown to the Poles by the farmers, sometimes even by Austrian guards. With rage it is noted that the rustic population had no aversion to the Polish soldiers, who were "not considered enemies but fellow Catholics." In some cases the villagers collected clothing and money for the POWs, who on occasion had to march without shoes. A complete lack of decency and fairness toward the defeated enemy is evidenced by various reports in which the SD complains that Poles received wine and cigarettes from the local population and were allowed to attend church on Christmas eve. What enraged the Nazis most of all was the fact that Austrian girls sometimes entered into intimate relations with Polish prisoners. From 1940 on POWs who committed that "racial crime" were executed. The girls were shorn of their hair, pilloried, and shipped to the concentration camp of Ravensbrück, where they were repeatedly flogged. This camp for female prisoners had been built in 1939 and turned into an inferno where the inmates were not only used as forced labor but also for medical experiments by a team of German physicians. Sick or infirm prisoners were gassed or killed by injections; on one occasion about 700 were killed in a day. The female prison guards were often more cruel than the men, and sadistic tortures like burying women up to the neck or pouring ice cold water on them in freezing weather were not uncommon.

Some inmates who were appointed "capos" managed to save other prisoners. A young Czech girl from Vienna, Anni Vavak, whose task it was to lead a column of prisoners to their daily work, was a shining figure of humanity in this place of horror.

While the day of reckoning with the Slavic nations was postponed, no such caution was deemed necessary with regard to the Gypsies, another minority that was considered racially inferior by the Nazis. Prejudice against that wandering nation had always been widespread; demands for their expulsion had been made as early as 1933. The Nazis decided to solve the Gypsy problem once and for all. At first the Gypsies were confined to the Burgenland, the easternmost part of Austria, which borders on Hungary. Once concentrated in this area, they became an easy prey for the SD. In April 1940 deportations to Poland started. Eventually the Gypsies were brought to Auschwitz and other death camps, where most of them perished.

The terror against certain religious sects was increased. The persecution was mainly directed against the Seventh Day Adventists and the International Bible Students or Jehovah's Witnesses. These religious groups rejected military service and maintained close connections with their coreligionists abroad. In December 1940 Anton Strezak, a member of Jehovah's Witnesses, was executed as a conscientious objector—the first of a great number of victims in Austria. During the first year of World War II, 1,917 Jehovah's Witnesses were sentenced to death in the Reich. The charge was always the same: corrupting the *Wehrmacht*. A far greater number of these sectarians, men and women, were shipped to concentration camps. Their quiet courage often impressed the other inmates.

A peculiar situation developed in South Tyrol, a part of Austria that had been annexed by Italy in 1919. Though the population was predominantly German by language and ancestry, Hitler made no attempt to claim their territory, for he wished to avoid a conflict with Mussolini. Instead he accommodated his ally by a cynical treaty concerning a transfer of population that was concluded in

October 1939. The inhabitants could either opt for emigration to the Reich or become true Italians. Of the South Tyroleans, 58% voted for "return to the Reich," but only about 80,000—a third of the total population—actually were resettled.[2] In the fall of 1941 the whole action ground to a halt; the Italians, whose military situation was deteriorating, had more important worries. In the meantime, no one knew what to do with the new arrivals. The governor of the recently occupied Crimea, an Austrian Nazi with a fertile imagination, suggested that the South Tyroleans be shipped to that part of Russia. Fortunately for the people concerned, the Crimea was reconquered by the Russians before this adventurous plan could be carried out.

In spite of so many violent events, social life in Vienna went on at a brisk pace. Baldur von Schirach established himself as a great patron of art and music. He wished to make Vienna attractive for Balkan visitors and personally invited his guests to sample the city's night life. Prostitutes often were employed by the Gestapo as useful informers.

For the theater a new general manager (*Generalreferent*) was appointed, one Walter Thomas, another German in a key position. His background was not impressive, but Schirach did not want an Austrian in so sensitive a job. Thomas was a fairly decent person, who eliminated the infamous stool pigeon Hartmann from the Burgtheater and occasionally tried to help actors who were Jewish or who in some other way were considered undesirable. He immediately came into conflict with Deputy Mayor Blaschke, who was a fanatical SS man but hated Prussians.

In his eagerness to stimulate Vienna's cultural life, Schirach initiated festivals in memory of great Austrian poets and composers. In a ludicrous manner they were always presented as German folk heroes, although this was in contradiction to historical fact. Many Viennese must have been slightly astonished when, for example,

[2] These figures are somewhat doubtful. According to other sources, only 64,000 persons left South Tyrol.

Franz Grillparzer,[3] Austria's greatest poet, was described by Schirach as a Pan-German. It would have been easy to quote from his works and arrive at very different conclusions.[4] Naturally, some local authors, for example, the poet Josef Weinheber and the novelist Bruno Brehm, were happy to serve the regime. Others, less enthusiastic, easily bowed to pressure. They had the ready excuse that writers were bound to their native language and would starve abroad. There were also some noteworthy exceptions like the poetess Paula von Preradovic, who was later imprisoned but survived. Another talented writer, Alma Johanna König, who happened to be Jewish, was deported and perished at Minsk. Her last novel, published long after her death, dealt—almost prophetically —with the Emperor Nero. Two other Jewish authors, the poet Jura Soyfer and the lawyer and novelist Heinrich Steinitz, also perished.

The writers, composers, and artists who willingly became Hitler's lackeys could point to some prominent colleagues in the Reich who had indeed set them a very bad example. Gerhart Hauptmann, doyen of the German drama, had long since declared his loyalty to Hitler. His early work had been of a pronounced socialist tendency, but the Nazis were in need of converts with a reputation and all was forgiven. In 1942, Hauptmann celebrated his eightieth birthday in Vienna and was widely cheered. Undoubtedly, vanity, the fear of losing his royalties, and old age were equally responsible for the aged author's attitude.[5]

A similar case was that of Richard Strauss, then Germany's greatest and most versatile living composer. Strauss lived in Bavaria but moved to Vienna in 1941 at the invitation of Baldur von Schirach. An unlikely convert to National Socialism, Strauss had a Jewish daughter-in-law and had worked with Jews during his entire career. Perhaps his cooperation with the Nazis was at least

---

[3] Franz Grillparzer (1791–1872) was the author of several tragedies dealing with historical subjects.

[4] For example: "The Prussian art of acquisition is like thievery during a blaze." Or: "The path of modern culture leads from humanity via nationality to bestiality."

[5] Predictably, after the war Hauptmann welcomed the Russians. He died in 1946.

partly dictated by the wish to protect his family. In Vienna, Strauss was treated as an honored guest, lived on a grand scale, conducted the Philharmonic Orchestra, and received the Beethoven award. His daughter-in-law and her two children remained unmolested.

Vienna's theaters were extremely active during the first phase of the war. There was certainly no lack of an audience, for most people were very glad to forget the war for a few hours. In strange contrast, long lines formed every morning in front of the Viennese prisons. These were mostly women who wanted to bring food and clothes to their husbands, sons, or other relatives who were languishing in jail. And while Herr von Schirach was making his pompous speeches on German culture and its European mission, strange things were taking place at Hartheim Castle in Upper Austria. Transports of insane, incurably sick, or crippled patients arrived and never left. The victims were shipped in regular post buses and unloaded in the courtyard. Then they were told to undress and walk into the "bathroom." That room was equipped with gas pipes that emitted poison gas. Three adjoining ovens worked day and night to consume the bodies. The remnants were loaded into trucks and deposited in the river Danube. That was Hitler's euthanasia program, an efficient process to destroy "biologically inferior persons." Similar installations existed in Germany, sometimes directly connected with homes for the mentally sick.

Hartheim fell under the administration of the camp commandant of Mauthausen. This made it possible to send sick or disabled camp inmates to the Hartheim gas chamber. They were simply shipped to the castle "for special treatment." Altogether about 30,000 human beings were liquidated at Hartheim. The population of the surrounding villages was probably well aware of what was going on because of the ghastly odor which emanated from the ovens as well as the bones and ashes which often dropped from the trucks.

What is really amazing is the fact that during the five years the euthanasia program was functioning, no physician in Austria raised his voice to protest. There can be no doubt that numerous doctors fully realized that their patients were being killed. The disappearance of so many inmates of various medical and mental institutions cannot possibly have gone unnoticed. Furthermore, the extermination took place not in faraway Poland but only 17 miles from the city of Linz. One can only conclude that the doctors were either too scared to dissent or agreed with the systematic liquidation of the victims.

Baldur von Schirach, Hitler's gentlemanly satrap in Austria, never showed the slightest inclination to mitigate the Nazi terror in Austria. Later, as a defendant at Nuremberg and in his memoirs, he disclaimed knowledge of the assorted horrors that were committed under his authority. His allegations do not deserve credence. A report of the German Department of Justice mentions that he was among those district leaders who never intervened for persons doomed to die. His colleagues in Salzburg and Lower Austria were not quite so merciless. It is interesting to note that Henriette von Schirach, the *Gauleiter's* lady, made a lone attempt to help the Jews during a visit to Hitler's retreat in Berchtesgaden. The Führer told her rudely to mind her own business. Her husband proudly took credit for the disappearance of the Jews at a Youth Congress in September 1942.

If Baldur von Schirach were ignorant regarding the fate of the deportees, he could easily have obtained information from an Austrian SS officer whom he frequently met at dinners and receptions. The name of this man was Ernst Kaltenbrunner. Until 1938 he had been a lawyer at Linz and an eager but not very well known supporter of the illegal Nazi Party. During the next years he rose in the ranks of the SS, but his name was rarely mentioned in the newspapers. A tall man of cold, aloof behavior, he was not one of the Nazi celebrities. Kaltenbrunner's hour came when Heydrich, chief of the SD, was assassinated in Prague. Kaltenbrunner became his successor, the only Austrian who rose to a high position in the Nazi government. In the last three years of the war he signed every order that referred to arrests, deportations, and special executions. During the period he was one of the most powerful men in German-controlled Europe. He must have been a worried police

chief in November 1942, because during that month the whole situation underwent a decisive change.

Within two weeks Rommel's Afrika Korps was defeated at El Alamein, the Allies landed in North Africa, and the Sixth German Army was encircled by the Russians between the Volga and the Don. The German news reports made light of these setbacks, but the casualty lists mounted in an alarming way. The disasters of Tunis and Stalingrad were still to come, but confidence in a German victory began to wane.

7
STALINGRAD AND AFTER

On February 2, 1943, the last remnants of 22 German divisions that had been encircled at Stalingrad laid down their arms. This time it was not possible to hide the plain facts of the debacle. Among the 90,000 soldiers who surrendered to the Russians were many Austrians. According to rumors, all German POWs were shot, but the Austrians were treated well. This was of course pure invention. Actually, only a few thousand prisoners survived; the majority simply died from injuries, exhaustion, and epidemics.

The police reported alarming incidents in Austria. When told that his son had fallen, a farmer tore a Hitler photo from the wall and threw it at the Nazi official who had brought the bad news. A woman informed of her son's death slapped a Nazi functionary's face. A Swedish journalist who visited Austria in early 1943 wrote: "Five years of German nationalist domination have revived the Austrian idea. . . . The Austrians reject not only National Socialism but German nationalism itself. The capital of old Austria is lost to the Third Reich. . . . Even Graz, once a Nazi bulwark, has thoroughly changed."[1] Hatred of the "Prussians" was now hardly disguised; the expression "Prussian" or "Piefke" was widely applied to everybody who hailed from the Reich. Even party members sometimes showed their aversion to the "German brethren."

Stalingrad changed the face of the war. Until 1943 the German government hesitated to impose strict austerities on the nation, especially on the privileged classes. The British had lowered the level of private comfort far more drastically and also employed a greater number of women in their armament industries. In Germany many leading party members and officials lived in great luxury. Others found convenient shelters in the occupied territories, where the German rulers adopted the ways of the parasitic proconsuls of imperial Rome. The immensely complicated structure of the regime led to waste and disorganization. The Germans relied to a large extent on forced labor from the subject nations and subsequently on troops from allied or occupied countries. Those often unwilling soldiers and workers became a liability in the last years of the war. In Russia and in the Balkans the guerrilla war had grown to alarming dimensions. By the end of 1942 the Yugoslav partisan armies consisted of about 150,000 men, and minor actions began to affect the borderland of Carinthia.

The dictatorship felt threatened and the terror was intensified. All through 1942 there had been arrests of malcontents, dissidents, and actual resistance fighters. But like the mythical hydra, for every severed head the growing discontent sprouted new ones.

Propaganda Minister Josef Goebbels appointed a special observer, one Egon Arthur Schmidt, to attend the trials before the People's Court. His reports are revealing. In Graz alone, 64 persons were in the dock within two weeks and 43 of them drew death sentences. At one trial in Vienna the defendant was carried into the courtroom on a stretcher. He had cut his arteries on the day before the session. In another case, the trial of a Socialist func-

[1] Awil Fredborg, *Behind the Steel Wall* (London: Harrap, 1944).

tionary, 8 of the witnesses for the prosecution were already under
sentence of death. Schmidt remarks that even the Nazis in the
audience were impressed by their brave behavior. Of course, witnesses and accused were all executed.

Meanwhile, Ernst Kaltenbrunner, the new chief of the *Reichssicherheitsamt* or RSHA (Reich Security office) grew into his job.
On several occasions he visited the concentration camp at
Mauthausen and attended executions of male and female inmates.
At the Vienna District Court the executioner Alois Weiss and
his aides were busy men. In that building alone 1,200 persons
were beheaded during the period of German occupation. The rising
number of executions in the armed services is revealing as well.
Daily life became more strenuous. Food rations were decreased and
many small business enterprises had to close because of lack of
raw materials. Church bells were confiscated as metal became
scarce. A number of children from the bombed cities of the Reich
were evacuated to Austria.

For the Nazi leisure class, life was still pleasant. Baldur von
Schirach acquired an elegant private home in a Vienna suburb.
The party functionary, Eduard Frauenfeld, not to be outdone, lived
in sumptuous style in another manor that had been confiscated
from a Jewish owner. Some of his colleagues complained to Berlin
about such wastefulness, but to no avail. Schirach himself was now
far from popular with the party leadership in Berlin. It was thought
that he spent too much money for unnecessary congresses. He was
also accused of meddling in foreign policy. Some of the art exhibitions that were sponsored by the Vienna district leader aroused the
ire of Goebbels, who considered the paintings *"entartet,"* the work
of degenerates.[2] However, no proper replacement for Schirach
was found, and he kept his position to the bitter end. The cultural
manager Thomas had to be sacrificed and was replaced by a Nazi
nonentity.

In the meantime, the underground Resistance received some un-

[2] An exposition of "Young Art in the German Reich" was closed prematurely
on orders from Berlin.

expected help from abroad. The Germans were constantly transporting foreign labor to Austria from the occupied countries. Control of the identity of these workers was not always very thorough. A certain number of young Austrians who had previously emigrated managed to slip back into their homeland with forged papers. Most of these clandestine returnees came from France and Belgium; a few had also served on the Republican side in the Spanish Civil War. They were young, dedicated people who returned in the full knowledge that their chance of survival was slight. They knew only too well that arrest meant months, even years, of ill-treatment and torture and eventually execution.

We shall briefly sketch here the life of one young girl whose political career is representative. Hedi Urach was born in 1916, the daughter of a Viennese streetcar conductor. She was arrested in 1938 for her Communist activities but managed to escape to Belgium. In spite of the great risk she returned to Vienna and was a member of the illegal underground organization when she was arrested by the Gestapo. Hedi Urach spent two years in jail awaiting trial and withstood all interrogations with fortitude. She refused to confess anything but was eventually sentenced to death on the testimony of others. She remained in the death cell for five more months and organized little farewell parties for those who preceded her to the scaffold. Two letters which this brave woman managed to smuggle out to her family have been preserved. In one of them she wrote: "Don't be sad; I am just a soldier of a good cause who has been called to duty."

A heroine of very different persuasion but equal courage was Sister Restituta, a Catholic nun. She was born Helene Kafka, a farmer's daughter and unlike Hedi Urach she was a mature person when she decided to fight the Nazis. As a nurse in the hospital at Mödling she aroused the anger of the Nazis when she refused to remove the crucifixes from the walls of the ward. In 1942 the hospital director denounced her for distributing anti-Nazi leaflets. These leaflets called for Austrian independence and urged young Catholics to refuse to serve Hitler. She was sentenced to death for "instigation for high treason" and beheaded five months later. Her father confessor characterized her in the following words: "She had a dynamic character and stood fearlessly for her belief and for justice. Servility and diplomacy were odious to her. For that reason the National Socialists were her sworn enemies. They just waited for the moment to deliver a mortal blow to her."

The complexity of Austrian politics can be judged from the fate of Richard Bernaschek. An ardent Socialist, commander of the Republican *Schutzbund* at Linz, Bernaschek had in 1934 opened fire on the troops of the Dollfuss government and actually started the civil war. He was captured, escaped to Germany, and for several years wandered all over Europe. When Austria was occupied by the Nazis, Bernaschek returned. In those days the Nazi leadership still hoped to win over the Socialists, so Bernaschek was only temporarily imprisoned. After his release he worked systematically to rebuild an underground Socialist movement in Upper Austria. In 1944 Bernaschek was again arrested and taken to Mauthausen, where he was shot a few days before the liberation.

It was the tragedy of the Austrian Resistance that for a long period of time it stuck to honorable but not very effective methods. These brave men and women collected money for the victims of the regime, wrote fine poems, and printed and distributed leaflets— an often fruitless and highly dangerous activity. The printing had to be done in the most unlikely places. An important distribution center in Vienna was located in a laundry. Others engaged in propaganda by letter, often directed to soldiers at the front. Undermining the armed forces was punishable by death, so the writers took an enormous risk. Much time and effort was devoted to spreading the news from Allied broadcasting stations, mainly the BBC. For most Austrians their radio set was the only tenuous link to the Allied world. At first the news was disseminated merely by word of mouth, but later on small news sheets were clandestinely printed. The British maintained several programs specially directed to Austria. The transmitters were located in England but pretended to be stations of the Austrian opposition. Unlike the regular BBC news, which was very reliable, these broadcasts provided a mixture of fact and fancy richly spiced with rumor and gossip. They may have encouraged the real underground, but were not very effective.

Only very gradually did the Resistance accept the more deadly techniques of sabotage and guerrilla warfare. That a well-organized dictatorship could only be shaken by hard, ruthless action was clear enough. Unfortunately, unified leadership with a specific aim in view was lacking. The opposition remained divided into many small groups. Another great difficulty was the absence of competent military direction and the lack of arms and explosives. Some small groups showed considerable ingenuity, like the one led by a gentle-faced, bespectacled chemistry student named Walter Kämpf. This resourceful young man had his comrades, many of them teenage girls, collect film scrap and other inflammable material that was fashioned into small incendiary bombs for acts of sabotage. Kämpf was also editor of an illegal newspaper, *Der Soldatenrat* (The Soldier's Guide), which called on the armed forces to give up the hopeless struggle. Military postal numbers were collected and the news sheet was sent directly to soldiers at the front. After a long investigation the Gestapo tracked down and arrested all members of the group. All were executed. Another team of saboteurs manufactured arrows that carried an incendiary substance. They managed to set several hundred army vehicles ablaze. However, in this case, too, all participants were caught and no one survived.

The Tyroleans have always been very independent people, and the whole province was honeycombed by illegal organizations of various political persuasions. Arrogant "Prussian" behavior, persecution of the Catholic Church, and resentment regarding the treatment of South Tyrol drove many patriots into underground opposition. Among the leaders were several Catholic priests. Six of them were caught and later executed.[3] A circle of intellectuals, the "Wednesday Group," did much to maintain the spirit of re-

---

[3] One of these priests was hanged by his feet at Buchenwald concentration camp until he died. The others were tried and executed. A memorial wall tablet at Stams Abbey commemorates the death of these martyrs.

sistance. The remote Ötztal became a refuge for persons who had to hide from the Gestapo. Here a solid nucleus of activists was formed under the leadership of Hubert Saurwein, "the Ötztal's Tito." By the end of 1943 a fairly well-armed band of resolute men existed in that mountainous area. The arms and ammunition came from army deserters or sympathizing police officers. Similar initial formations of partisans turned up in Styria and Carinthia. The Germans recorded growing activity of "bandits" who attacked farms and factories. By March 1942 the word "partisans" was eliminated from all reports because the Germans feared—quite correctly—that it gave their enemies a heroic stature.

The persecution of the Slovene minority drove more and more young men into the partisan groups across the border. In April 1942, 300 Slovene families were suddenly rounded up and expelled from their homes. Most of them were deported to Germany, but a certain number managed to escape into the mountains. They were later joined by Austrian resistance fighters and deserters from the *Wehrmacht*. Meanwhile, Yugoslavia became the scene of intensified warfare. By the fall of 1943 no fewer than 21 German divisions were tied down in the Balkans.

A particularly sensitive area was Upper Styria with the industrial towns of Donawitz and Leoben. The region had a strong Socialist tradition, but there were also many Nazis, and the big steel factories were closely watched by the Gestapo. In Leoben a special commando of the SD had the task to combat the Resistance. A troop of selected bully boys was maintained in the factories to keep the workers, among them many POWs, under control. The whole region was crawling with army and SS units. Still, the underground was growing and infiltrated many government agencies. Telephone operators and railroad personnel often provided important links for the Resistance and warned of impending police actions. Weapons were stolen from armament dumps with the cooperation of Austrian soldiers who sympathized with the anti-Nazi movement. In a later chapter we shall discuss the Austrian partisan movement.

The Germans were fully aware of the fact that opposition was increasing. By 1943 all higher positions in Austria were occupied by Germans and to a lesser degree by fanatical local Nazis. Of course, to a certain extent this policy was bound to be counterproductive. Many Austrians who in 1938 had been favorably inclined toward the Reich felt frustrated by 1943. They had expected a better future in an enlarged Germany, and had no desire to be treated as a colonial population. After Stalingrad the number of Austrians who were well disposed toward Germany diminished steadily, but the majority remained inactive, either out of fear or simply out of indifference. These people had never wanted war and found the prospect of a *guerre à l'outrance*, a fight to the finish, depressing. Furthermore, the fronts—Russia and North Africa—were still far away and Austria had not yet suffered any major air attacks.

However, there was one subtle change, not yet very visible at that time. In the army, in prisons and concentration camps, former political adversaries met and realized that they were all together in a desperate situation. They shared dire peril, ill-treatment, and humiliating conditions. They knew that their wives and children were living in constant anxiety. They heard of neighbors who had been deported and never returned. They saw their compatriots being sacrificed by the thousands in a war they never had desired. They saw men go to their death because they had refused to bow to a cruel and arrogant despotism. Gradually, a new sense of solidarity developed, a longing for freedom and independence. The first stirring of a new Austrian patriotism occurred mainly in the camps, where the inmates experienced the very depth of human misery.

8
THE TURNING POINT

On May 13, 1943, the Axis forces in Tunis surrendered. In July an Allied invasion fleet appeared on the coast of Sicily and in September the Italian mainland itself became a theater of military operations. The fall of Mussolini was overshadowed by his rescue from captivity; an Austrian SS officer named Otto Skorzeny appeared as the conquering hero.

What all that meant in military terms became clear to the Austrians on August 13. In all of Lower Austria the wailing of sirens announced the arrival of a new enemy from the skies, the US Air Force. In Vienna only a distant grumbling was heard, but 33 miles to the south 187 tons of bombs fell on the industrial town of Wiener Neustadt, home of a large aircraft factory. When the bombers left, the plant was in shambles, about 200 persons lay dead in the ruins, and a full passenger train was ablaze at the railway station. The air war had finally reached Austria. The American planes had started from their base at Bizerta in Tunis. However, a few weeks later the Allies captured the airfields at

Foggia in Southern Italy and all future raids were made from that airbase, which was greatly enlarged. By December 1943 about 35,000 air force personnel were stationed at Foggia and Bari.

The air war against targets in Austria proceeded slowly. In 1943 the Allied main effort was still directed against western and northern Germany. Austria never experienced anything comparable to the raids against Hamburg, which left about 50,000 persons dead within 10 days. However, the growing danger from the skies forced the Luftwaffe to regroup its forces. A large number of fighter planes had to be shifted to bases in Austria and Bavaria, and consequently these were missed at other theaters of war. Thousands of new anti-aircraft guns (88 mm) were positioned in Austria. In Vienna, large, ugly concrete towers were built which bristled with guns.[1] In 1943 Vienna was attacked from the air only eight times. Other raids were directed against Klagenfurt and Innsbruck. The British method of intense night raids, which might well have broken the already shaky morale of the population, was not practiced in Austria. Vienna was not yet a prime target, but the era when the war was far away had ended. Another consequence of the collapse of Italy was a more intensive war in Yugoslavia, where the Italian occupation troops had to be replaced by Germans. Some Italian units even defected to the partisans.

In Austria the alliance with Italy never had been popular, due to painful memories from World War I. The older Austrians remembered that Italy had defected to the Allies in 1915 and generally reacted to the new situation with the remark: "I told you so." Of course, the Nazis pointed out that the Allies had now merely gained a foothold and had won no decisive victory. The slow and far from spectacular Allied advance in Italy seemed to confirm that point of view. For Hitler's adversaries in the occupied countries, the Italian campaign was disappointing.

By contrast, the events in Russia raised hopes that the Nazis were faltering. After an unsuccessful German offensive at Kursk,

---

[1] They were so massive that they could not be dismantled after the war and still survive.

the initiative passed to the Red Army. From Orel, which fell on August 5, to Vienna and Berlin was still a long way, but from that date on the Soviet armies never stopped advancing. Japan, so successful in 1942, was now clearly on the defensive. The battle of the Atlantic was still in full swing; here too the tide was turning against Germany.

The far-flung German armies became more vulnerable due to supply problems. The railroads were vital to them and sabotage was increasing. Among the Austrian railway workers were many foes of the Nazis. There were constant arrests and hundreds of railroad employees were executed.

The Germans made an enormous effort to keep the "fortress Europe" under full control and to build up their armament industries. Simultaneously, the growing unrest in all occupied territories led to an enormous intensification of the terror. In autumn 1942 Roland Freisler was appointed presiding officer of the People's Court. Freisler was a former Communist who had defected to the Nazis and tried to outdo his colleagues in brutality to make his masters forget his compromising past. A letter by this "hanging judge" to the German Minister of Justice has been preserved. Writing shortly after his appointment, Freisler points out that Communism and high treason were rampant in Germany and "especially concentrated in the Alpine and Danube districts," meaning Austria. In the courtroom Freisler behaved like a bloodthirsty bully, heaping scorn and abuse on the defendants. Obviously, he derived a sadistic pleasure from sending men and women to the gallows or the scaffold. Some death sentences pronounced by this tribunal would be simply incredible if the full records had not survived. A few examples will suffice here. Freisler's career came to an end when an American bomb fell on the Berlin courthouse in February 1945, killing him instantly.

One seventeen-year-old girl was beheaded because she wrote letters to 50 soldiers urging them "to stop the slaughter." Soon people were also executed for minor infractions like stealing property of the armed services or looting after air raids. Petty offenses that would normally have been punished with a few weeks in prison were now capital crimes. One young girl went to the scaffold because she had stolen cigarettes from an army parcel. Father Johann Schwingshackl, a Tyrolean priest, was sentenced to death because he had written a private letter to his superior in which he described National Socialism as a danger to religion. Though he suffered from tuberculosis and intestinal bleeding, he was kept in chains. In his last letter he expressed satisfaction that he was dying as a martyr for his beliefs. The execution did not take place, for he died of natural causes in the death cell. Another Tyrolean, Johann Vogl, a school principal, wrote: "The People's Court wears red robes and caps, red as blood, the symbol of that tribunal. The prosecutor is a Prussian, the presiding officer is a Prussian; I think that tells the whole story. For a Tyrolean there is only one expectation: a bitter death." The charges against Vogl were far from clear; it seems that he had sought some contact with German Socialists, and that was quite sufficient to seal his fate. His son, a soldier in the *Wehrmacht*, tried to intervene with the Tyrolean district leader Franz Hofer, but to no avail.

The spirit of the resistance fighters remained unbroken in spite of all torments. The following letter, written by Emil König, a Socialist streetcar employee, to his son was smuggled out of prison.

My dear son Helge,
I do not know where I will be on your 13th birthday, so I write you today. I ask your mother to forward this letter to you on your birthday. . . .

There has been a great crisis in human society all over the world. Unemployment, poverty, and misery weighed heavily on many people. Your parents felt this too, although we were both employed. But we always had a social conscience. In spite of these conditions there was free speech and freedom of thought. No one was imprisoned because of his opinion about the solution of these problems. And there was peace! Brother did not fight brother. There were no destroyed cities, no broken hearts. So it went until you were four years old. Then, for the first time, guns were fired and the freedom of the workers and of most people was crushed. The few who had property and wealth begun to rule. Freedom of speech and opinion was abolished. Your father stood always in the ranks of those who fought for justice and liberty. Mother and you, my two sons, are my dearest ones. However, ethics and ideals force me to stand up for them to the last. You should always be aware of that, my son! It is painful to say so, but it is right and you should make that your life's principle. . . .

My words are grave, your father lives in a difficult situation, but in spite of all I remain firm and straight. Your father loves you and your brother deeply and truly, so reflect upon his words and pass them on. Your father kisses and embraces you.

(signed)
Emil König

König wrote two more letters to his wife and his two sons one hour before his execution. He remained fearless and calm, his last thoughts full of concern for his family.

The report of the public prosecutor Lautz in which charges against 244 defendants are mentioned is revealing. Lautz continues: "The number of Marxist traitors who are known to the secret state police is far higher." He goes on to explain that to arrest them all is impossible because there are not enough jails. Besides, production in important plants like the railroads would be endangered if all these men were imprisoned. This certainly proves that opposition was by then fairly widespread.[2]

As the war continued, the procedures of the courts became more perfunctory. The lawyers were hardly given time to study the charges against their clients. They merely went through the motions of a defense. One of these court-appointed attorneys openly told his client: "I am a Nazi. I refuse to exert myself for a Socialist!"

Many details regarding the fate of political prisoners can be found in the reports of Hans Rieger, Protestant chaplain at the Vienna *Landesgericht* (district court). He established contact with

---

[2] Lautz's report is dated October 3, 1942, prior to the fall of Stalingrad and the upsurge of resistance.

many inmates who were to be executed. Because sending food to those prisoners was strictly prohibited, the unfortunates were often near starvation. Despite that ban, the Reverend Rieger risked his own freedom and smuggled food parcels into the cells. His good offices went to all in need, no matter what their political or religious persuasion. He fully deserved the title of "guardian angel of the condemned."

On one occasion a Catholic theology student was to be executed. Out of sheer inhumanity the judge refused the condemned man the consolation of his priest. The Reverend Rieger willingly replaced his colleague, heard the delinquent's confession, and accompanied him on the way to the scaffold. In most other cases the Catholic chaplain, Monsignor Eduard Köck, was allowed to assist prisoners of his faith. However, the crucifix had to be removed from the room where the culprit faced the court prior to his execution. During the last three years of the war, clergymen were forbidden to pray while the hangman was doing his duty. In spite of all this petty harassment, most of the condemned went to their deaths bravely.

The number of foreign laborers in Austria was constantly growing while more and more young and not-so-young men were drafted into the armed forces. A large number of workers came from the occupied parts of the Soviet Union, but there were also Frenchmen, Italians, and even Spanish Republicans from the internment camps of France. A number of industrial plants employed POWs and even political prisoners as forced labor.

The Nazi leadership in Vienna made a determined effort to keep the cultural life going. In 1943 one could still go to the opera, to the theater, or to a concert and enjoy fairly good performances. Naturally, the movie houses were playing, and although most of the German films were atrociously bad they found large audiences, as everybody was grateful for a little distraction. Vienna's German mayor Jung quietly vanished and was replaced by his deputy, Hanns Blaschke, who mixed his ferocious orations with a strange brand of local patriotism. The Austrian Nazis at least had the satisfaction that one of their own crowd was now master at City Hall.

In the armed forces the Austrian officers rarely got above the rank of major or colonel. Only one, General Lothar Rendulic, reached prominent status, although on the rather remote front in northern Norway.[3] In the air force one Austrian, Alexander Löhr, made it to colonel general and later had the thankless task of directing the retreat from Yugoslavia.[4]

We have already mentioned SS *Obersturmbannführer* (a rank that is equal to colonel) Otto Skorzeny, who rose to fame as Mussolini's rescuer and was subsequently used for special daredevil assignments. We shall encounter him again in Vienna, with the Red Army at the gates.

For the great mass of Austrian soldiers who were drafted, there was no particular glory. They did their duty and hoped to survive. Undoubtedly, many were quite aware of the fact that they were actually serving a cause that was not their own, but it was extremely difficult to escape from that duty. During the last two years of the war, desertion increased; in a later chapter we shall describe the consequences.

One of the symptoms of total war was a certain leveling off concerning the general living standard. With the exception of the small party and army hierarchy, social differences were reduced. Luxury vanished or at least retreated from public view. The party agencies made an effort to make the cultural life as inexpensive as possible. At the same time fear of future air raids led to a transfer of art treasures and archives to less endangered locations, like the old castles in Lower Austria.

---

[3] Rendulic commanded the 20th Mountain Army first in Finland, later in Norway. His reputation was tainted by the "rape of Finnmark."

[4] In 1947, Löhr was executed in Yugoslavia as a war criminal.

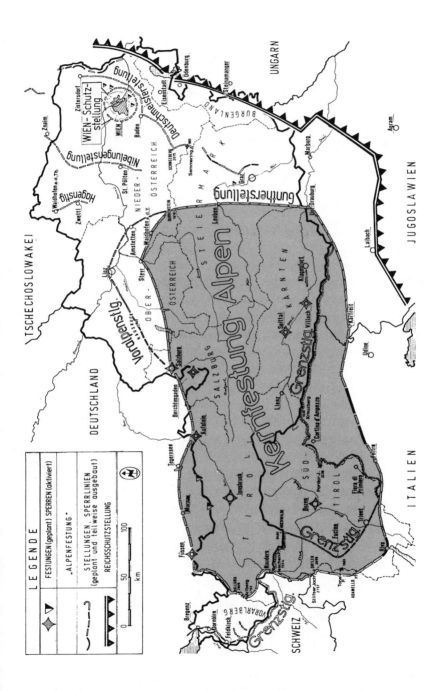

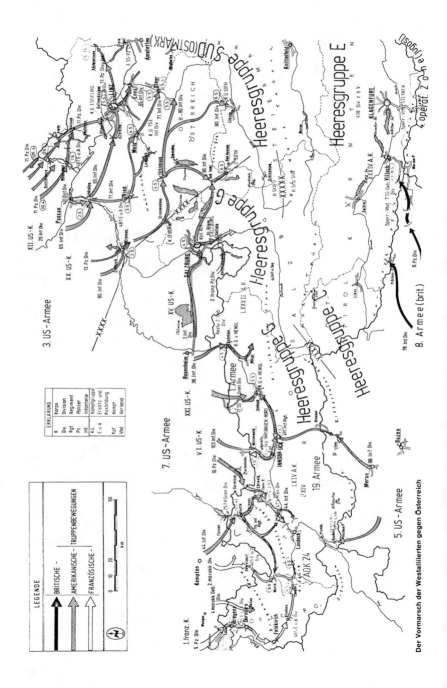

Der Vormarsch der Westalliierten gegen Österreich

Hitler's speech in Vienna before a crowd on the Heldenplatz.

Photo 1, 2 and 3 by courtesy of Time Inc.

The former Austrian Department of Defense right after the German occupation. The officers leaving the building still wear Austrian uniforms but the swastika flag has already been raised.

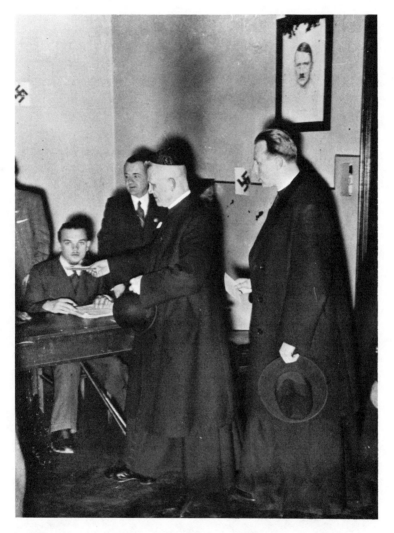

Cardinal Innitzer casts his vote for the Anschluss.

German infantry parades across the Ring in Vienna.

Photos 4–14 by courtesy of the Documentation Archiv of Austrian Resistance in Vienna.

Frontier gate at the Austrian border is removed.

Jewish boys are forced by Nazis to deface Jewish-owned stores.

Political prisoners in Dachau. The man to the right, Alfons Gorbach, became Austrian chancellor in 1961.

Mauthausen concentration camp in Upper Austria.

o 5, symbol of *Austria's independence*, painted on the wall of St. Stephen's cathedral in Vienna.

Mauthausen liberated by American troops.

Vienna after an Allied air raid. The Albertina museum in ruins.

Major Karl Biedermann's body swings from a lamp post. He was one of the last victims of the Nazi regime.

*The bridge over the river Enns where Americans and Russians met on
May 8, 1945.*

Independence after seven years of Nazi rule. Chancellor Karl Renner (left) and Mayor Theodor Körner walk to the parliament building to proclaim the new Austrian Republic.

9
THE AUSTRIANS ABROAD

The Austrians who played a political part in other countries must be divided into two categories: those who were sent by Hitler to govern the occupied territories and those who had emigrated. The first group consisted only of a few individuals. However, their record is such that history cannot ignore it.

We have already mentioned that Hitler preferred using the more prominent Austrian Nazis outside of their homeland. The biggest position went to Arthur Seyss-Inquart, the "historical telephone operator" of the *Anschluss*. After a short tour of duty in Poland, the man who had betrayed Schuschnigg became the highest official of the Reich in the occupied Netherlands. He governed the country for five years, and his reign of blood, plunder, and degradation will not soon be forgotten.

Outwardly, that bespectacled lawyer who limped and spoke in a monotonous voice seemed insignificant. However, he was highly intelligent and a persistent climber. It is interesting that Hitler came to appreciate his services to such a degree that in his last will he appointed him Minister of Foreign Affairs. Seyss-Inquart could not assume this high office; his career ended with imprisonment and eventually the hangman's noose in Nuremberg.

When Seyss-Inquart moved to the Hague as Commissioner of the Reich (*Reichskommissar*), he was accompanied by three Austrians: Hanns Albin Rauter, Friedrich Wimmer, and Hans Fischböck. All three were high SS officers; Rauter bore the title of "Higher SS and Police Chief," a rank equal to general. He was the man who forged the instruments of terror and was directly responsible for the deportation of more than 100,000 Jews, the rounding up of approximately 300,000 Dutchmen as forced labor, the pillage and confiscation of property, and a large number of murders and executions as reprisals against the Dutch Resistance.

Rauter's career was symptomatic of the men who came from the most radical wing of the Austrian Nazi party. Born in Klagenfurt and a veteran of World War I, he had twice commanded volunteers who fought against Yugoslavians and Hungarians in the turbulent postwar era. Then he became a leader of the *Heimatschutz* in Styria, a fascist organization that eventually turned Nazi.[1] When the latter was banned, Rauter left Austria and became a German citizen, organizing an Austrian legion in Germany. After the *Anschluss* he returned to Austria. Unlike the colorless Seyss-Inquart, Rauter was an outright fanatic—in the words of his superior, "a big child with a child's cruelty." His personal reign of terror came to an end when he was seriously wounded in an encounter with the Dutch Resistance in March 1945. After Germany's surrender, Rauter was arrested in a German hospital, extradited to Holland, and executed in 1949 as a war criminal.

We have already mentioned Odilo Globocnik, briefly district leader of Vienna in 1938, later one of the main executors of the "Final Solution." In stark contrast to Rauter, who never enriched himself, Globocnik was a thoroughly corrupt individual. His reign in the district of Lublin (Poland) became such a scandal that he

---

[1] Outside of Styria, the *Heimatschutz* or *Heimwehr* opposed the Nazis. Rauter and his followers were dissidents.

was transferred to Istria. He committed suicide when the Third Reich collapsed.

Gustav Otto Wächter was a man of very different caliber. He was a lawyer and the son of a former Austrian Minister of Defense. In 1934 he had directed the ill-fated coup d'état against the Dollfuss government. He escaped to Germany, but his further career was hurt by that conspicuous failure. At the outbreak of the war he was transferred to Poland to govern the province of Galicia. His behavior in that occupied zone was relatively moderate. He attempted to win the Ukrainian population for Germany, but in 1944 he was again transferred, this time to Trieste, Italy. When Germany surrendered, he fled to Rome, where he died a few months later.

Alfred Eduard Frauenfeld had a colorful career. He had played an important part in the early days of the Austrian Nazi party. He performed the function of *Gauleiter*[2] until he fled to Germany, where his violent diatribes against the Austrian government preceded the assassination of Chancellor Dollfuss. When the first Nazi putsch failed, this type of propaganda was discontinued and Frauenfeld was moved to a position in the field of Nazi culture. In 1942 he was sent to the Crimea as "general commissioner of Tauria." It was he who suggested that the South Tyroleans be transferred to that zone of occupation. A memo concerning occupation policy which Frauenfeld sent to Berlin shows him in a relatively favorable light. He called the German treatment of the Russian population the "zenith of lunacy" that drove those people into partisan warfare. He pointed out correctly that the Germans in the Crimea were greeted as liberators but within one year lost that goodwill by their brutal behavior. Frauenfeld's reign ended abruptly when the Soviet armies recaptured the Crimea in May 1944. He returned to Vienna and for a while was under consideration as Schirach's successor. The arrival of the Red Army put an end to such ambitious plans.[3]

[2] He used this title at a time when Austria was still independent.
[3] His brother Eduard Frauenfeld was also a high Nazi functionary.

Edmund Glaise-Horstenau was one of those respectable Nazis who were used by Hitler to infiltrate the Austrian government in 1936. Predictably, he openly worked for the *Anschluss* when the chips were down, but the Nazis held no high opinion of him and he had to be content with a diplomatic post in Zagreb, Yugoslavia. In his memoirs he admitted that the events of World War II had turned him into a "fanatical Austrian." His change of mind came too late to be of use to anybody, and in the end he took his own life.

Political emigration from Austria started as early as 1934, when the Dollfuss government put down the Socialist uprising. Several hundred of the Viennese fighting force escaped to Czechoslovakia. Otto Bauer, the intellectual leader and theoretician of the Social Democratic Party, died in 1938 in Paris, a defeated man. Julius Deutsch, who had military experience, fought in the Spanish Civil War, escaped to the United States, and eventually returned to Austria after the end of World War II. The rank-and-file refugees, mostly members of the Republican *Schutzbund*, were offered asylum by Soviet Russia. At first they were welcomed as heroes, but when Stalin started his great purge in 1936 most of them disappeared into the Siberian labor camps. A few, like the journalist Ernst Fischer and his striking, aristocratic wife, remained unmolested and served the Soviet Union all through the war with fierce dedication. Like the British, the Russians made special broadcasts to Austria, and efforts were started to persuade Austrian soldiers to defect to the Red Army. However, desertion at the front was highly dangerous, and many soldiers feared—and with reason—that the Russians would not be particularly kind toward anybody in German uniform.

Large-scale emigration began only with the German occupation; for the most part it was dictated by Hitler's racial policy. We have already mentioned that about 128,000 Jews left Austria from 1938 to 1942. Most of them were not political refugees in the conventional sense, nor did they represent a uniform group. They encompassed almost every profession and differed widely with regard to their background and political opinion. In contrast to the emigrés of the French and Russian revolutions, they even lacked a common ideological bond. Most of them were impecunious and faced the necessity of earning a living in a foreign country. Only a very few turned to politics, and their influence on future events was very limited.

A number of Austrian politicians managed to escape from the Nazis; later they were joined by other dissidents. Some Austrian diplomats refused to serve the Reich and simply stayed abroad. The Austrian ambassador Georg Franckenstein was made a British subject and even raised to the nobility, but he refused to form an Austrian government in exile, for he knew only too well that no nation would have recognized it. A few members of the defunct Schuschnigg government, for example, Minister Guido Zernatto, eventually turned up in the United States, but they could not exert much influence.[4]

The only person who could have functioned as an Austrian leader in exile had left Austria shortly after the end of World War I, when he was a little boy of six. Otto von Hapsburg-Lothringen, son of the last emperor, was indeed the legitimate heir of the monarchy. He was a serious, well-educated young man who had been brought up in Belgium. He had been in close contact with Schuschnigg, who was a monarchist at heart but far too cautious to restore the Hapsburg monarchy. Shortly before the *Anschluss*, Otto had in fact offered himself as Austrian chancellor to form a united front against Hitler. In 1940, after the fall of France, he appeared in Washington and began to agitate for a Hapsburg restoration, a future federation of the smaller European countries as a counterforce against Germany and the Soviet Union. For a short time he found some sympathy in Britain and the United States, but it was feared that a restored Austria with the borders of 1918 would be too weak. The idea of some sort of Central European federation was repeatedly discussed. However, there was great opposition to such a project from the Czech and

[4] Zernatto, who was also a gifted poet, died in New York in February of 1943, at age 39.

Italian exiles, who had no wish to see the Hapsburgs in power again. The Allied governments approached the Austrian question with extreme caution. In September 1942 Foreign Secretary Anthony Eden replied to an inquiry in the House of Commons that his government did not feel bound by the events of 1938. Even as late as May 1943, Winston Churchill spoke of "a Danubian confederation with Vienna at its center." A clear declaration for the independence of Austria was as yet lacking. An effort to raise an Austrian battalion within the United States Army came to nothing.

It is noteworthy that even among the Austrians in exile there seemed to be no consensus of opinion. Julius Braunthal, an Austrian Socialist living in London, declared in August 1943 that unification with Germany was Austria's right, although it would be wiser not to exercise it. Many Socialists of the old generation had grown up with the idea that the *Anschluss* itself was not objectionable as long as Germany had a democratic, preferably a Socialist, government. They were very slow in giving up that notion, especially if they lived abroad and did not feel the Prussian heel upon their throats.

One group of Austrian Socialists had taken refuge in Sweden. They were all younger men, and unlike their friends in England and America they always maintained a certain contact with their homeland. Sweden was a neutral country, travel was still possible, and the Swedes did a brisk business with the Reich. Furthermore, Sweden allowed German troop transports to pass on to the Finnish front. Therefore, contact with Austrian soldiers was sometimes possible for the refugees. Under those circumstances the refugees in Sweden were well informed about what was going on at home. They were aware of the fact that the Austrians were cured of any earlier predilection for the Reich. This view is clearly noticeable in a proclamation that one of these young men addressed to all Socialist organizations in the West. The writer's name was Bruno Kreisky.[5]

---

[5] Austrian Federal Chancellor since 1970, previously Foreign Minister.

Most tragic was the fate of the refugees who had emigrated to European countries that were later occupied by the German army—France, Belgium, and the Netherlands. Since these refugees held German passports, they were considered enemy aliens and frequently interned. After the fall of France, the Gestapo had no difficulty identifying them, and in 1942 they were earmarked for deportation. Those who were known for anti-Nazi activity had already been arrested at an earlier date. Only a small number could hide with the aid of the Resistance movement—no easy matter because their foreign accents usually made them conspicuous. A certain number of Austrian refugees found an uncertain refuge in unoccupied France. In spite of the shameful and cowardly behavior of the Vichy government,[6] there was a better chance to survive south of the demarcation line. When the Germans occupied Southern France in November 1942, the French Resistance was already fairly strong and many Austrian refugees and deserters joined it.

Austrian soldiers who were eager to defect to the Allies often found contact with the underground. Several Austrians served with great distinction in the FFI (*Forces Françaises de l' Intérieur*). Conditions for joining the French Resistance were relatively favorable, as the movement was widespread and the general attitude of the population was hostile toward the occupying power. By the fall of 1942 the great majority of Frenchmen, Belgians, and Dutchmen were convinced that Germany was losing the war, and their willingness to collaborate with the Germans was constantly diminishing. In France a secret organization, TA—*Travail Anti-Allemand* (Anti-German Work), was formed; many Austrians belonged to it. They printed leaflets in German, distributed them among the occupation troops, and transferred Resistance fighters from France to Austria—a very risky undertaking which few survived.

---

[6] The Vichy government delivered thousands of foreign refugees to the Germans. Foreigners who had volunteered for the French Army in 1939 were deported to labor camps in Africa, where many perished.

The Gestapo was so worried about these activities that a special team of interrogators was sent from Vienna to Paris. For a full year these sleuths were unsuccessful. In 1944, shortly before the liberation of Paris, they arrested an Austrian nurse who named a few names under severe torture. The unfortunate young woman committed suicide by jumping from a sixth floor window of the prison at Fresnes. Her confession led to a number of further arrests in France and Austria. As a consequence, five men and two women who belonged to her organization were executed in Vienna.

Among the Austrians who worked for the French Resistance was a group of very young girls who were quite effective in intelligence work and anti-Nazi agitation among the *Wehrmacht* soldiers. In the other occupied countries the number of Austrians was too small for any coordinated action. They could only join native resistance movements as individuals or in very small groups. A young Austrian, Karl Gröger, took part in a daring attack on the public office of registration in Amsterdam. The Resistance fighters were disguised as Dutch policemen. They were later apprehended and executed. The same fate met five Austrian soldiers who had joined the Norwegian underground. Tragically, this also led to the execution of an Austrian priest who had received correspondence from one of the men but was quite ignorant of his friend's activities in Norway. A most remarkable figure was Monsignor Otto Gramann, Catholic chaplain at the Belgian fortress of Breendonk, where many freedom fighters were kept imprisoned. He had been an Austrian cavalry officer in World War I, and the Nazis may have thought that a soldier turned priest would be more sympathetic to their cause than the average cleric. However, Father Gramann was completely on the side of the Belgian patriots who were tortured and executed at Breendonk. He accompanied many of them on their last walk to the firing squad.

Altogether, about 10,000 Austrians fought on the Allied side against the Nazis. The number of those who joined in various foreign resistance movements is difficult to ascertain, for most of them did not survive. The activities of Austrian volunteers in the Yugoslavian army will be discussed in a later chapter.

The Allies finally did resolve to make a clear declaration with regard to Austria's independence. This document, jointly signed at Moscow by Cordell Hull (US), Anthony Eden (Great Britain), and Vyacheslav Molotov (USSR), was published on November 1, 1943. It declared that Austria, the first victim of Hitler's aggression, must be liberated from German domination.

The *Anschluss* was declared null and void and all changes of law made by the Germans as not binding for the Allied governments. Austria was to be restored as a free and independent state. However, it was also reminded of the inescapable responsibility which it bore for participating in Hitler's war. In the final reckoning, the part Austria itself would play in its own liberation would be considered.

The Moscow declaration was confirmed by the Big Three at their conference in Teheran four weeks later. During this meeting Joseph Stalin emphasized that Austria had existed independently and could do so again. He did not believe in a Danubian federation and pressed for independence of all smaller nations in that area. Probably he was already planning to keep them separate but control them and eventually form his own economic and military *cordon sanitaire* against the West.

Naturally, the Austrians heard about the Moscow declaration via the BBC. It cheered those who were in opposition to Hitler anyway, but did little to influence the majority of the population at that time. The Allies were still far away, engaged in a very slow advance in southern Italy. The Soviet armies had reached Kiev, but in those days most people believed that Austria would eventually be liberated by an Allied thrust from the Adriatic. This idea was indeed very much on Churchill's mind; he envisaged an offensive from the head of the Adriatic toward the so-called Ljubljana Gap and farther into Austria. Such a "stab at Germany's Adriatic armpit" was repeatedly under discussion but eventually was abandoned in favor of a landing in the South of France. The idea was once more debated at the second Quebec Conference in September 1944 with an eye to forestalling the Red Army in Austria and Hungary. Again that operation, which might have changed the whole political situation in Central Europe, was rejected.

On the day the Moscow declaration was published, more than 100 American bombers renewed the attack on Wiener Neustadt. The Americans lost 17 planes, but the damage they caused was so great that industrial production in that area was reduced by more than 50%. Unbeknownst to all but the men at the top, the disintegration of Hitler's New Order began to affect his lesser allies. Hungary and Romania, after having suffered grievous losses at the Eastern Front, were secretly negotiating with London. The Hungarian prime minister Miklos Kallay was in fact quite willing to surrender to the British if they could only reach the frontiers of Hungary. King Boris of Bulgaria died suddenly and mysteriously in August 1943.[7] Growing unrest flared up in his country, which had always refused to fight Russia. Outwardly the Germans were still masters of the Balkans. Some thoughtful Austrians remembered that the disaster of 1918 had started in the Balkans.

[7] It was rumored that he was poisoned after a visit to Hitler's headquarters. He was only 49 and in good health. If the Germans killed him, they did not improve their position in Bulgaria by that murder.

10
THE ROOTS OF CONSPIRACY

For ten years Nazi Germany had shown the world the strong face of a monolithic autocracy. Whatever opposition had existed to the Hitler regime seemed to have been eradicated completely. As to the German army, it was fighting a losing battle with undiminished vigor. The German people still seemed to follow their Führer with boundless confidence. In spite of the series of defeats suffered during 1943, the Reich still presented the image of a nation united in arms.

This appearance was somewhat deceptive. Twice, during the Czechoslovakian crisis and again in November 1939, the generals came very close to revolting against Hitler. On both occasions they lost courage at the decisive moment. The military opposition was led by the former Chief of the General Staff, Ludwig Beck, a man of honor but hardly of action. After the great military victories of 1940, conspiratorial activity came to a standstill, but it revived after the Stalingrad disaster. A growing number of younger officers joined the opposition. The real leadership now passed to Count

Claus Schenck von Stauffenberg, a one-eyed, one-armed veteran of the Afrika Korps, later Chief of Staff of the Home Army with the rank of colonel.

The basic plan of the conspirators was to assassinate Hitler and immediately place the Reich under the control of the army. The new government, composed partly of military men, partly of civilians, was to arrest the prominent Nazis, immobilize the SS and the Gestapo, and start negotiations with the Western powers for an armistice.

It is not within the scope of this book to tell the full story of the conspiracy which eventually led to the ill-fated attempt on Hitler's life on July 20, 1944, and ended in complete disaster. Rather, we shall concentrate on its connections and consequences in Austria. It all started with a meeting of two Germans and three Austrians at Vienna in October 1942. The Germans were two prominent civilian conspirators, Carl Gördeler, previously mayor of Leipzig,[1] and Jakob Kaiser, former chairman of the Christian labor unions. The Austrians were Lois Weinberger, also of the Christian labor movement and an old acquaintance of Kaiser's, Otto Troidl, and Felix Hurdes.

Gördeler, for all his antagonism to Hitler, was an old-time German nationalist who believed in a "Greater Germany" that included Austria. When Gördeler developed his ideas to the three Austrians, Weinberger replied: "We shall gladly do everything to help you. But let us in the first place be what we have been for so long: Austrians!" The conversation established contact between the German and Austrian opposition but had no direct results.

In May 1943 another spokesman of the German Resistance, the Socialist Wilhelm Leuschner, came to Vienna. He contacted one of the leading Social Democrats, Adolf Schärf,[2] the former secretary of Vienna's renowned ex-mayor Karl Seitz. Leuschner, too, believed that Austria should remain a part of a democratic postwar Ger-

---

[1] Gördeler resigned as mayor of Leipzig because the Nazis had removed the monument to the Jewish composer Felix Mendelssohn.
[2] Schärf became President of Austria in 1957.

many. He was taken aback when Schärf told him abruptly: "The *Anschluss* is dead. The Austrians have been purged of any love for the German Reich!" The somewhat shaken German emissary also spoke to Weinberger and Hurdes and got a similar answer. The position of the Austrian underground was quite clear: They were willing to help their German counterparts in overthrowing Hitler, but Austria had to be independent. The Moscow declaration of November 1, 1943, confirmed their views.

The German opposition was slow in realizing the Austrian position. For a time they even pondered the appointment of Kurt von Schuschnigg as Minister of Education in their future cabinet. The Austrian ex-chancellor was a prisoner at the Oranienburg concentration camp after having been dragged through three different prisons. Since December 1941 his wife had been allowed to share his confinement, and they were permitted to inhabit a little house within the camp under constant guard by the SS. The poor man had no contact with the outer world and was greatly surprised when he heard about those plans—after the war.[3]

In 1944, Kaiser had another conversation with Weinberger and Hurdes. The deadline for a German coup d'état was approaching and Kaiser wanted the names of prominent Austrian politicians who could be named as delegates when the new government was to take power. After some hesitation, the names of ex-mayor Karl Seitz and of the senior agrarian spokesman, Josef Reither, were mentioned. Later the name of Franz Rehrl, former governor of Salzburg, was added. However, these three men were not part of the actual conspiracy; they were merely known to be loyal Austrians and democrats. The fact that the conspirators knew their names was later the reason for their arrest, and they were fortunate to escape execution.

We must now return to Berlin, where the officer's plot against Hitler was gradually taking shape. During the fall of 1943 no fewer than six attempts were made to murder Hitler. However,

---

[3] Schuschnigg regained his freedom in May 1945.

the Führer seemed to have a charmed life; in every single case the plans miscarried. On one occasion a bomb placed in his plane failed to explode. Another attempt came to nothing because of an Allied air raid, and on several other occasions Hitler simply did not appear where he was expected.

Meanwhile the military conspirators had hit on a seemingly perfect plan for taking control once the Führer was safely out of the way. An official plan to halt potential unrest within the Reich was in existence under the code name "Operation Valkyrie." In such an emergency the Commander of the German Home Army was to take over. Sealed envelopes were issued to all military districts containing instructions in case Valkyrie orders were to be signaled via teletype. Here was the perfect instrument to put a total army coup d'état into effect. Colonel Stauffenberg and his immediate superior, General Friedrich Olbricht, were in key positions to launch the critical operation. "Valkyrie," designed to suppress revolution, was to be used for the purpose of a military putsch.

It was a brilliant and daring plan, but its execution depended on many uncertain factors. It had to checkmate the Nazis all over the Reich and in the occupied territories. Any delay could have fatal consequences. Hitler's headquarters had to be completely isolated to avoid any contradictory orders. The dissident generals at central headquarters in Berlin had to be firmly established before the Nazis could start a counteraction.

One of Stauffenberg's closest subordinates was Lieutenant Colonel Robert Bernardis, the most prominent Austrian officer within the conspiracy. Bernardis had originally served in the Austrian army and was transferred to the *Wehrmacht* in 1938. Like many naive young men he had believed in Hitler's "Greater Germany," but the deception was only a temporary one. Bernardis was too intelligent and too civilized to remain ignorant of the true character of National Socialism. He joined the conspiracy, and it became his task to make contacts with Command (*Wehrkreis*) XVII, meaning Austria.

The leading military conspirator in Vienna was Colonel Rudolf von Marogna-Redwitz, former chief of German counterintelligence (*Abwehr*) in Munich. Having served in the old Imperial Austrian Army and later in the German Army, Marogna became a close collaborator of Admiral Wilhelm Canaris, the famous head of the *Abwehr* and one of Hitler's most persistent adversaries. In 1938 he was transferred to Vienna and often held a protective hand over those who were persecuted by the Nazis. Tragically, both his sons died at the front, fighting for a system their father abhorred.

A few words must be added here concerning the *Abwehr*, as this organization formed a pillar of the military resistance. For nine years (1935–1944) it was commanded by Wilhelm Canaris, one of the most interesting and enigmatic personalities of that era. The "little admiral" was a convinced anti-Nazi, but certainly also a German patriot. He has been called the "Hamlet of conservative Germany." He warned the victims of Nazi aggression, helped to smuggle Jews out disguised as *Abwehr* agents, and staffed his command with men of the Resistance, among them Erwin Lahousen, previously of the Austrian General Staff.[4] In fact, it was the fall of Canaris that drove the conspirators to speed up their actions. The *Abwehr* had long been suspected of treasonable activities by Kaltenbrunner. In February 1944, several *Abwehr* agents defected to the British, and shortly afterwards Canaris was deposed by Hitler. His organization was absorbed into Kaltenbrunner's Security Service (RSHA).

The fall of Canaris, the penetration of a peripheral group of the conspiracy by the Gestapo, and finally the arrest of Julius Leber, one of the leading German Socialists, proved that the plot could not remain secret any longer. The conspiracy had spread too far. Further arrests would reveal the plot, and so the decisive strike against the regime could not be delayed without endangering all concerned.

---

[4] Lahousen was one of the few survivors of the conspiracy. He appeared at Nuremberg as a witness for the prosecution. His evidence was highly damaging to the defendants.

Furthermore, the military situation had gone from bad to worse. The Russians had taken Odessa and Sebastopol, and the shadow of the Red Army began to fall over the Balkans. Hungary's position had become so uncertain that the Germans occupied the country on March 19, 1944, to prevent its defection. The vital Romanian oilfields were now within range of the American air force. In Italy the Allies advanced on Rome, which fell on June 4. Two days later the Normandy invasion breached the Atlantic Wall. That new crisis increased the pressure for action on the reluctant conspirators. Every new defeat decreased their chances for negotiating a favorable armistice with the Allies.

In July the crisis deepened. Stauffenberg, who had access to Hitler, failed on two occasions to detonate his bomb. On July 17 Field Marshal Erwin Rommel, who was a late and somewhat reluctant convert to the conspiracy, was seriously wounded during an air attack. On the same day the Gestapo issued a warrant for the arrest of Carl Gördeler, who was designated by the plotters as the new chancellor of the Reich.[5] Beck and Stauffenberg decided that a new attempt on the Führer's life would be made on July 20 during a conference at the *Wolfsschanze*[6] at Rastenburg.

According to the plan, the Chief of Communications, General Erich Fellgiebel, would promptly cut off Hitler's headquarters after the explosion. The generals in Berlin would then issue the code word Valkyrie, arrest *Gauleiter* Goebbels, and have the SS in all military districts disarmed. In Vienna there were actually only two officers who were full-fledged members of the conspiracy: the aforementioned Colonel Marogna-Redwitz and Captain Karl Szokoll. A third one, Lieutenant Colonel Robert Arenberg, was an active sympathizer. Bernardis was in Berlin, busy composing the resumé that his chief Stauffenberg was to present to the Führer at Rastenburg. These papers and the bomb traveled together in Stauffenberg's briefcase.

---

[5] Gördeler escaped arrest but was later caught and executed.
[6] The "Wolf's Lair," Hitler's headquarters in East Prussia, about 50 miles behind the front.

Marogna-Redwitz, who was related to Stauffenberg and who had recently lost his job at the *Abwehr*, had been appointed by the latter to inspect several army units in Hungary and Slovakia. On the morning of July 20 he arrived in Vienna ready to act in a commanding function once the government was in the hands of the Berlin conspirators. But fate was to intervene once more in Hitler's favor.

11
JULY 20, 1944

The events that took place in Berlin and Rastenburg on July 20, 1944, often have been described by competent historians.[1] We shall review them only briefly to explain what happened in Vienna a few hours later.

At 12.32 P.M. Colonel Stauffenberg, briefcase in hand, entered the conference barracks at Rastenburg. He shoved the briefcase with the time bomb under the table about six feet from the spot where Hitler stood. Then he left the room. By pure chance another officer pushed the briefcase away. The bomb exploded at 12:42 P.M., wounding him and three other men fatally. Hitler was only slightly injured. Stauffenberg saw the barracks go up in flames with a roar. Bodies and debris were hurtling out of the windows. Convinced that Hitler had been killed, Stauffenberg and one of his

[1] See H. B. Gisevius, *To the Bitter End* (Boston: Houghton Mifflin, 1947); F. V. Schlabrendorff, *The Secret War against Hitler* (New York: Putnam, 1965); J. W. Wheeler-Bennett, *The Nemesis of Power* (New York: St. Martin's Press, 1954), and many others.

accomplices jumped in his car and managed to pass all checkpoints, although an alarm had already been sounded. He raced to the nearby airport and his pilot took off immediately. He reached the Rangsdorf airport near Berlin at 3:45 P.M., still convinced that his fatal mission had been successful.

The first failure was followed by a second one. General Fellgiebel promptly called Berlin headquarters and informed his fellow conspirators that an explosion had taken place, but the connection was bad and whether Hitler was dead or alive remained in doubt. The plotters preferred to wait for Stauffenberg's arrival and let three precious hours pass. But, far worse, Fellgiebel did not succeed in cutting off the Rastenburg communications center. The reason has never been given; perhaps he was prevented from doing so by the SS. In any case, Hitler's headquarters remained in contact with Berlin. This had disastrous consequences for the conspirators. It was 4 P.M. when the codeword Valkyrie was finally flashed to all military district commanders. But at about the same time, a phone call to Rastenburg revealed the awful truth, namely, that Hitler was very much alive. Perhaps the conspirators could still have saved the day by immediately occupying all ministries and particularly the Gestapo headquarters and the Berlin broadcasting station. However, the unexpected setbacks threw everything into confusion. The armed troops that should have been used in Berlin did not appear. The officer who should have arrested Goebbels defected to the Nazi side when confronted with the fact that the Führer was far from dead and in fact was most eager to destroy his adversaries. In the end the very same soldiers occupied the War Ministry in the Bendlerstrasse and arrested the plotters. Stauffenberg and three others were immediately executed by firing squad, Beck shot himself, and Bernardis and several junior officers were caught by the SS. A wave of suicides and arrests followed.

In Vienna, July 20 was completely uneventful until 6 P.M. By sheer accident the two leading personages were out of town. Baldur von Schirach was attending his mother's funeral at Wiesbaden in Germany. General Schubert, the commander of military district

XVII, was peacefully vacationing, as were many other Viennese. His deputy, General Hans Karl von Esebeck, was a new arrival and unfamiliar with conditions in Austria. He had just left for dinner at the officers' mess when the first teletype from Berlin arrived.

The officer left in charge was Colonel Heinrich Kodré, chief of the general staff at the Vienna command. He was a good Austrian, no friend of the Nazis but not a member of the conspiracy. The only officer in the *Wehrkreis* building on the Stubenring who was aware of the plot was Captain Karl Szokoll, head of the organization section.

It was Kodré who received the decoded teletype message. Its text informed the local commander that because of interior unrest he had to take over all government powers within his district; police and SS forces were made subordinate to his command. The message spoke of "an unscrupulous group of party leaders" who were stabbing the fighting front in the back. For this reason the army had assumed responsibility "in this hour of supreme peril." The message was signed by Field Marshal Erwin von Witzleben, one of the main conspirators at Berlin. This puzzled Kodré, because he recalled that this senior officer had been retired from active service in 1942. However, Kodré hastened to call his superior, General von Esebeck. Even before that gentleman could return to his post, a second, more comprehensive teletype message arrived. It ordered that all Nazi officials, including the leaders of the SS and the Gestapo, must be promptly arrested and replaced by army personnel. The appointment of political delegates would follow in due course. Faced with a completely unexpected and most serious situation, Kodré flashed the Valkyrie code and ordered the Vienna town commander General Adolf Sinzinger and several other senior officers to come to his office. The latter was an old National Socialist who had been involved in the putsch against Dollfuss in 1934.

The general confusion was increased by the news broadcast of the German radio that an attempt on Hitler's life had failed.

Kodré called headquarters in Berlin and got Stauffenberg's personal confirmation that he should proceed with the arrest of the Nazi bigwigs. It was now decided to order them to Esebeck's office and detain them on the spot. A number of minor functionaries were arrested by General Sinzinger. The fact that an old Nazi like Sinzinger obediently executed orders that must have been most puzzling to him proves that the Valkyrie plan was basically a sound one. All seemed perfectly legal, and German officers were, after all, used to following orders without asking questions. The plot could have succeeded had the chief conspirators in Berlin acted with greater speed and audacity. The coup d'état failed at its very center in Berlin. In Vienna, Prague, and Paris it would have been completely successful.

At 8 P.M. Schirach's deputy Karl Scharizer, Eduard Frauenfeld, SS General Rudolf Querner, the two highest Gestapo functionaries, and two other SS officers were assembled. Esebeck told the men politely that they were under arrest. They were confined in several rooms, where they were served food and brandy. None of them offered any serious resistance, the two Gestapo leaders being too astonished to utter more than a verbal protest. The building was now under armed guard. By an extremely simple operation the whole Nazi leadership had been rendered completely powerless. Meanwhile, all strategic positions in the city were occupied by regular troops. The population hardly noticed anything unusual. After five years of war the presence of armed soldiers at railroad stations and post offices surprised no one. Besides, it was a very hot summer evening, and most people had taken refuge in the cooler parks and suburban inns. For about three hours the army was in full control of the city.

A third teletype from Berlin named former mayor Karl Seitz and Josef Reither as political delegates and Colonel Marogna-Redwitz as contact officer for Command XVII. Kodré, increasingly puzzled, conferred with Esebeck, to whom the names of Seitz and Reither meant nothing. However, the wily Frauenfeld became suspicious, and when a fourth teletype claimed that Hitler was dead, he shouted: "Something is wrong here, Colonel! The Führer is alive, I sense it!"

The turning point came at 11:20 P.M. with a phone call from Field Marshal Wilhelm Keitel at Rastenburg headquarters. Keitel, Hitler's obedient servant, roared that all orders from Berlin were "mystifications," that Hitler was alive and that he would have Colonel Kodré court-martialed. The unfortunate Colonel had no choice but to release his prisoners. Captain Szokoll, the only full-fledged conspirator among those nonplussed officers, made a last desperate attempt to reach Stauffenberg by phone, but their conversation was interrupted. About one hour later Stauffenberg was shot in the courtyard of the War Ministry in Berlin, while Bernardis and several others were led away handcuffed to prison.

Outside Vienna the whole action had not been noticed. In Salzburg the Valkyrie operation never got off the ground. The local army commander was busy playing cards and took no action.

The next morning the Nazi terror raced to apprehend the guilty, the suspects, and a number of perfectly innocent persons. Baldur von Schirach returned to Vienna in a fine rage and made General Sinzinger, who had been completely ignorant of the plot, his scapegoat. The general had his golden party badge torn off and was shipped to a concentration camp. The same fate was meted out to Colonel Kodré and several other Austrian officers who had merely obeyed orders from Berlin. Kodré survived in Mauthausen, where he was eventually liberated by American troops. Marogna-Redwitz was too deeply involved to escape the death penalty. His friend Lieutenant Colonel Arenberg was more fortunate: he was released after nine weeks, for the Gestapo thought him blameless. Even more astonishing is the fact that Captain Szokoll, the most dangerous Austrian conspirator, remained unmolested. He had covered his traces well and was to get his second chance against the Nazi regime in April 1945. The military plotters in Germany were all caught in the orgy of Hitler's revenge. The first batch of eight defendants, among them Witzleben, Olbricht, and Bernardis, appeared on August 7 before the People's Court in Berlin, with Judge Freisler presiding. They had already been expelled from the army by a so-called Court of Honor. Consequently, they wore no uniforms but were forced to appear in court in shabby civilian clothes without belts and collars. The trial itself was a grotesque mockery of justice. Freisler heaped insults on the accused, and the counsels for the defense seemed to aid the prosecution. The sentences were never in doubt.

Bernardis made no serious effort to defend himself. His last request, to be executed by a firing squad, was refused. As Stauffenberg's intimate friend he was doomed from the start. All eight defendants were hanged at Plötzensee prison under revolting circumstances. They were stripped and slowly strangled by piano wire thrown over meathooks. The executions were filmed so that the Führer and his staff could enjoy the agony of his adversaries. Bernardis, a sick man, went stoically to his death.

This was but the beginning of a series of mass executions. Among the more prominent victims were Admiral Canaris, General Fellgiebel, and Carl Gördeler. Field Marshal Rommel was forced to commit suicide; several others took their lives to avoid trial and execution. A far larger number of persons were imprisoned, among them all the relatives of the leading conspirators.

For Austria's opposition, the defeat of the conspiracy had serious consequences. The Gestapo arrested every person in its files who was even vaguely suspected of anti-Nazi activities. Off to jail went former mayor Seitz, agrarian leader Reither, and others who were supposed to have been in contact with the plotters. Actually, none of these men had been active in the conspiracy. They were lucky to escape execution. A great number of other suspects, mostly older politicians, were also sent to concentration camps. This policy of putting so many prominent suspects behind bars had an unexpected effect. The Nazis themselves laid the groundwork for a growing solidarity between Austrians of the most diverse backgrounds and political convictions.

There was no hope for those who were awaiting judgment for

illegal activities, even if these were quite unconnected with the July conspiracy. In March the small but effective group of the Catholic chaplain Heinrich Maier had been arrested. For two years they had passed important information to the Allies via Switzerland and Turkey. The data were mostly obtained by Father Maier, who moved in military circles, and sent abroad by Franz Josef Messner, the director of a large rubber company with international connections. Maier and his friends were no impractical idealists. They realized that an effective underground had to work with the Allies and that the most important contribution would be military information, particularly with regard to targets for the British and American bombers. Since February 1944 the air raids had been greatly intensified. Compared to the early Resistance groups, Father Maier and his circle represented a far more competent organization. The case reached the People's Court only after the July plot and ended with eight death sentences. After long and cruel imprisonment the men were finally beheaded three weeks before the liberation of Vienna and their naked bodies thrown into a mass grave at the Central Cemetery.

The July events radicalized the regime and strengthened its commitment to total war. The Home or Reserve Army was placed under Heinrich Himmler, a deliberate humiliation of the *Wehrmacht*. Four weeks after the Rastenburg explosion, Goebbels announced "total mobilization." All men between the ages of 15 and 60 could be drafted into the *Volkssturm*, a militia that proved of doubtful value. On September 1 all theaters, academies, and a number of vocational schools were closed. Even music schools and orchestras were disbanded, for Vienna a specially hard blow. Only the Vienna Philharmonic Orchestra and some radio music bands were exempted from that regulation.

The production of armaments was still mounting, thanks to the ingenious Albert Speer, a great organizer and improvisor. But the air war took its toll, and production of fuel dropped alarmingly. The Allied air force began to concentrate its attacks on oil refineries, five of which were located near Vienna. As early as March 1944, an intensive air raid had been directed against those factories and oil storage tanks. Soon the city itself, with its many widely dispersed armament and chemical plants, became a target for strategic bombing. On May 29 an unexpected air raid caused a number of chemical factories and many other buildings to go up in flames. On June 16 no fewer than 658 American bombers, protected by 290 fighter planes, attacked various targets in Austria. In St. Pölten alone 600 persons lost their lives.

Altogether, Vienna experienced 82 air raids during 1944. Gradually strategic bombing was replaced by fairly indiscriminate bombardment to break the morale of the population. The war had finally reached the home front, a fact that put an end to many illusions. And in the East the Russian steamroller, after some temporary delay, now rumbled toward the Romanian border. This coincided with another Allied invasion in Southern France.

The summer of 1944 saw for the first time a large-scale evacuation of children from Vienna to safer territories. The number of desertions was on the rise. The district of Goldegg, about 40 miles from Salzburg, was a hideout for many deserters. In July the SS blocked the whole area for an intensive manhunt: a number of villagers who aided the fugitives were arrested and several were even killed.

Under those circumstances it is remarkable that the great majority of the population remained indifferent. This was not exclusively due to terror, although the draconic punishments meted out to relatively minor offenders certainly deterred the more timid souls. In Vienna alone 47 women were executed for all kinds of trivial offenses.[2] The German propaganda was still quite successful. For the credulous there was still the hope of some miraculous new weapon that would suddenly change the fortunes of war. Hitler's

---

[2] Most of these unfortunates had stolen property belonging to the *Wehrmacht* or had engaged in black-market deals. Three of them were beheaded for being abortionists.

vaunted V-weapons had not caused very serious damage to the Allies, but their propaganda value for German morale was considerable.

Ironically, the destructive Allied air raids also provided grist for Goebbels' propaganda mill. It told the people who had lost all their property that a German victory was their only chance to gain compensation. The fact that any possible hope of conquest was long gone seemed not to matter.

The strongest argument of the Nazis was fear, in particular fear of the consequences of a Russian triumph. With the approach of the Soviet armies to the Balkan peninsula, that threat seemed real enough, and there is no doubt that it caused many Austrians—by no means only National Socialists—to continue to fight or at least not to turn against the German army. Too many people were now aware of the atrocities committed by the Nazis in the occupied territories. The idea that Russian troops would take savage revenge on their enemies was by no means unrealistic. The Nazis cleverly fed that fear by explaining that in case of a Soviet victory the whole population would be transported to Siberia. The uneasiness was not exactly diminished when the first fugitives from the Balkan front began to appear in Vienna.

12
THE KALTENBRUNNER REPORT

August 1944 was one of the most eventful months of World War II. In the West, Paris was liberated and the bulk of the German armies in France were destroyed. Romania abruptly changed sides and Bulgaria quickly followed suit. This brought the important oilfield at Ploesti under Russian control and forced the Germans to extricate their forces from Greece. Within days the whole strategic situation in the Balkans had completely changed. In Poland the Russians were held at the Vistula, but in the North the exhausted Finns sued for peace. Of the Reich's allies, only Hungary and the shaky puppet states of Croatia and Slovakia, both riddled by partisans, remained.

Still, Germany did not collapse. The armies maintained their habitual discipline in retreat. The fronts in the West and the East had been greatly shortened, while the rapid advance of the Allies delayed the arrival of Allied transports and supplies.

The German opposition had been liquidated in a sea of blood. The conspirators of July 20 had no support among the population and the lower ranks of the army. German morale remained high, as the Allies were soon to discover at Arnhem and in the Ardennes.

In Austria the situation was different. A very lucid report by Ernst Kaltenbrunner, dated September 14, 1944, draws a fairly accurate picture. The great security chief had personally traveled through his homeland and been alarmed by what he saw and heard.

Kaltenbrunner may have been a monster of cruelty, but he was by no means a fool. Hitler was convinced of his loyalty, but there are indications that the coldly calculating police chief would have liked to leave the sinking ship. He merely could not make up his mind how to go about it.

"Vienna is filled with despondence," wrote Kaltenbrunner. "The attitude of almost all classes of the population requires immediate action." He then went on to criticize the plans that were made for a line of fortifications in which none of the planners had the slightest confidence. The only result was to create a scare among the nervous city dwellers that, Kaltenbrunner noted, "could soon turn into panic." Comparison with Eastern Prussia, which was resolutely defended, was unfounded. Vienna lived in terror of the British and American "air gangsters" and feared that Hungary would defect and turn Communist. There was little hope that the German troops retreating from the Balkans would even reach Vienna. (Indeed, few of them did.) This defeatist mood made people receptive to all kinds of hostile propaganda and marked a trend toward Austrian independence. Kaltenbrunner seems to have visited several factories and working-class districts, and he called his impressions "definitely unpleasant."

So far the report is entirely correct. It becomes less so when Kaltenbrunner arrives at his conclusions. He clearly wanted to undermine Schirach and replace him with his protegé Frauenfeld; therefore he blames the "untenable situation" on the former and praises the latter. In reality, Frauenfeld was mainly a bluffer and a profiteer and would have failed in any case. It must be said in fairness that even a genius could not have prevented the approaching disaster.

Kaltenbrunner also worried about the district leader of Lower Austria, Hugo Jury, whom he considered too old and in poor health. However, Jury held very different opinions. He blamed the conditions in Vienna on the large percentage of "persons of foreign blood" among the inhabitants. Jury meant the descendants of "various Balkan nations" and the Czechs. He also feared the foreign laborers, who already numbered 140,000. However, Jury agreed with Kaltenbrunner that Schirach was a total failure, a society gentleman without executive ability. His conclusion was that Vienna and Lower Austria should be fused into one unified district with himself, Hugo Jury, as *Gauleiter*. Hitler rejected his proposal. That fusion of districts smacked of Austrian separatism.

A third secret report came from Schirach's own deputy, Karl Scharizer. Probably he had his own self-serving reasons for discrediting his boss, but his remarks have the ring of truth. He described Schirach as "a nobleman, a baron, he does not know the value of money . . . lives in another world for his own hobbies . . . cannot identify with the way of life of little people." What angered Scharizer and his cronies most was not Schirach's incompetence, but the fact that he employed no fewer than 17 chambermaids. Scharizer added gleefully that Mayor Blaschke, too, was a total failure. "A typical cultured snob, he knows nothing of administration," Scharizer commented. This he followed with a most unflattering description of five other Nazi bigwigs. Like Jury, Scharizer was frightened of foreign laborers, especially the French, who were turning intractable.

Clearly, the relations among the Nazi leaders within Austria were deteriorating. It is not known what the Führer thought of these various reports about his *Gauleiter*. Schirach was not deposed and remained at his post until his flight in April 1945.

With the collapse of Germany's southeastern front, Vienna became flooded with refugees: ethnic Germans from Romania and Yugoslavia, collaborators fleeing from their former domiciles, even a Bulgarian government-in-exile. Slovakia, often praised as the Reich's model satellite, suddenly revolted, and for almost two months a bloody partisan war raged in the Carpathian Mountains. The Russians were slow in advancing in that region, and the Germans suppressed the Slovak uprising before the Red Army could reach the important mountain passes. Older Austrians reminisced with mixed feelings about 1915, when the armies of the Czar had been held at bay in the rugged Carpathians. But in the Balkans the Russian advance continued. The Hungarians gladly would have followed the Romanian example, but it was too late. Admiral Miklós Horthy was forced to abdicate in 1944 and was taken in custody. The fight had to go on. There were rumors that Vienna was to be declared an open city, but the story was angrily denied by Mayor Blaschke.

The Allies had long ago ceased to treat Vienna and other Austrian cities with consideration. Their main intention was to cripple industry and transportation. From September 1944 on, the air offensive was vigorously intensified. The German fighter squadrons resisted with great valor and the 15th US Air Force suffered serious losses. However, the Germans began to feel the scarcity of fuel, which was aggravated by Romania's defection. For that very reason the Allies concentrated on the domestic refineries, but a number of bombs fell on densely inhabited city districts. According to official figures, a raid on Vienna on September 10 killed about 700 persons, but the actual casualties were probably higher. Many raids were clearly directed against specific targets, like oil refineries and railroad stations. Nazi propaganda declared all raids to be "terror attacks" destined to break the morale of the civil population. If this was the Allies' intention, they succeeded in Austria far better than in Germany. The population's anger at the growing destruction turned mainly against Hitler and his henchmen. By fall 1944 it was clear to everybody except totally besotted fanatics that the US Air Force could operate above Austria with little restraint. The schedule of the air raids on Vienna was almost uniform. The bombers started from Italy in the morning and entered Austria after having formed themselves into attack formations above Western Hungary. The fighter escort engaged the Luftwaffe which operated from nearby airfields. The first warning of approaching bombers, popularly called "the cuckoo," was given by radio. The center of Vienna possessed extended subterranean shelters, and cautious people who were not working, like housewives and elderly persons, tried to stay in nearby parks. Schirach and his staff habitually raced to the command bunker via the long Thaliastrasse, mockingly called "Avenue of Final Victory." Around noon the American squadrons reached the city area, the sirens wailed, the bombs began to fall, and the gun towers fired on the raiders. Those attacks took place with such regularity that many families took their Sunday lunch at 10:30 A.M.; at noontime they expected to be in the shelters. In contrast to the tactic used in Germany, the RAF did not undertake any night raids on Vienna, and the city did not suffer the fearful "fire storms" that razed Hamburg and Dresden. Nevertheless, whole streets changed into rubble, and people got used to living behind broken and barricaded windows in a permanent atmosphere of smoke and dust. For hours they had to sit in ice-cold shelters and basements while the buildings collapsed and the earth shook under the explosions. In December the first Russian planes appeared over Austria, but they usually devoted their efforts to observation.

We have already mentioned the growing unrest in Styria, Carinthia, and Tyrol. In 1944 partisan warfare had engulfed many parts of Europe and tied up large numbers of occupation troops. The partisans, fully familiar with their rugged terrain, proved to be more than a match for regular troops, who had to move in difficult and hostile territory. In Yugoslavia, the partisans, well supplied by British airdrops from Italian bases, controlled vast parts of the country.

In Austria the partisans remained essentially confined to a few remote alpine regions. Larger military operations were not possible because there were not enough arms and supplies. The partisans were small groups of resolute young men who engaged in "hit-and-run" tactics. They could never hope to defeat superior military units, therefore they had to avoid any major engagement. When faced with well-equipped forces, they retreated to their mountain hideaways. Their main object was the disruption of traffic, slowing down supplies for the front and creating confusion among army and police units. Some groups operated shortwave transmitters and provided information for the Allies.

It was not a gentleman's war. The partisans faced a foe who burned farms, tortured prisoners, and took ferocious reprisals against the families of opponents. Civilians who carried arms or explosives could not expect mercy when caught. The atrocities committed by the SS in Styria and Carinthia were almost beyond description. Naturally, the partisans could not exist without a degree of aid from the local population. We shall cite only one case to illustrate the reprisals taken against such sympathizers. A farmer in Unterpetzen, Carinthia, was suspected of helping the insurgents. The SS not only killed him but mowed down all persons living on his farm with machine gun salvos and burned the building to the ground. Among the victims were several small children. Similar massacres and the persecution of the Slovene minorities drove many young men and women into the ranks of the partisans. Contact was made with Tito's troops across the border. Two of the activist leaders of the Leoben group served for a short time with Tito's forces in Slovenia, where they gained some practical experience. In July 1944, their group fought a sharp engagement with regular German troops at the Thalerkogel near Trofaiach and narrowly escaped destruction. A few days later they derailed a supply train right in the town of Leoben. These men, mostly miners and steel workers, were armed with weapons pilfered from German ammunition dumps. During the last phase of the war, the partisans sometimes were reinforced by Allied paratroopers and an occasional airdrop of arms. However, these reinforcements remained on a small scale.

In Carinthia the main center of partisan activity was the rugged area of the Koralpe, not far from the Yugoslavian border. Among these resistance fighters were men who had served in the Spanish Civil War and with the Allied armies. They were joined by Austrian deserters and Slovene refugees. Austrian and Yugoslav partisans cooperated in the border region. On one occasion an SS battalion chasing the Austrians was ambushed by the Yugoslavs and lost 180 men. The Germans tried again and again to gain control of the Koralpe strongholds but never succeeded. Another small partisan unit built a formidable redoubt in the Steinerne Meer ("sea of stones"), an isolated mountain region in southern Carinthia. Two attempts by superior forces to dislodge the defenders were repulsed with heavy losses for both sides.

Gradually many Austrians crossed the border into Yugoslavia, where eventually five Austrian battalions were formed. Numerous POWs who decided to fight against Hitler joined these units. During the last four months of the war, one of these battalions was constantly in action in the border region.

Compared with the great battles going on in 1944 and 1945, the activity of partisans in the Austrian Alps was of minor importance. However, these pinpricks made the German authorities extremely nervous and forced them to assign more SS and police units to a critical area that was declared a *"Bandengebiet"* (guerrilla area). How serious the threat of partisan warfare was considered is made clear by a report of the Styrian *Gauleiter* Siegfried Uiberreither. Ordered to build a defense line in his district, he demanded reinforcements, and for good reason. "Two-thirds of that defense line," wrote the harassed district leader, "runs through guerrilla regions."

13
O 5, CODE FOR FREEDOM

Walls in Vienna, Innsbruck, and other cities began to show the figures "o 5," drawn with chalk or paint during the night. Leaflets which read "Freedom— o 5—Austria" appeared on the streets. o 5 meant *Oesterreich* (Austria), the 5 standing for "E," the fifth letter of the alphabet. Very soon the people—and the Gestapo too—realized that the figures were the new symbol of the Austrian Resistance.

For six years the underground had been systematically drained of its leading personalities. The loss of so many potential leaders was one of the major reasons for the lack of systematic, unified organization. The great wave of arrests after July 20, 1944, sent almost all older politicians who had still survived to the concentration camps. Despite all the efforts of Kaltenbrunner, his spies, torturers, and hangmen, the underground had found new leaders, however. It was finally decided to coordinate various Resistance groups and to form a central committee that became known under the name of POEN (*Provisorisches Oesterreichisches National-komitee*, Provisional Austrian National Committee). It consisted at first of six members: Ernst Molden, Heinrich Otto Spitz, Alfred Verdross, Josef Etzdorf, Friedrich Maurig, and Major Alfons Still-fried.

Ernst Molden's sons, Fritz and Otto, were also very active in the Resistance.[1] Fritz Molden had founded an underground group in Italy and developed contacts with the Italian partisan movement. However, his activities were discovered and two of his co-workers were executed. Molden himself fled to Switzerland, where he set up a new center. It served as a link with the Austrian underground and with Allied intelligence in northern Italy. A secret courier service across the Italian-Swiss border near Lake Como began to function. An Austrian underground office in Milan made contact with Allen W. Dulles, chief of the OSS (Office of Strategic Services) in Bern.

In September 1944, Fritz Molden, disguised as a German ser-geant, visited Vienna and Innsbruck and contacted the leading Resistance organizers. Closer cooperation between the Austrian underground and the various Allied intelligence services became reality. Couriers began to operate in the mountains at the Swiss-Austrian border. Good contact was established with the French, and this was promoted by the fact that a number of Austrians were already serving with the French armies. One of these officers, Ernst Lemberger (Captain Jean Lambert), joined Fritz Molden on one of the latter's secret missions to Vienna. They met with the POEN leaders and were appointed to represent this organization for negotiations with the Allies. Plans were made for more direct aid from abroad in the form of airdrops. However, the Gestapo was still very much alive, and in February 1945 most POEN members and other Resistance fighters suddenly were arrested.

---

[1] They both published memoirs of those years; see the bibliography. Their father was a noted journalist and their mother, the celebrated poetess Paula von Preradovic.

Among those imprisoned was Hans Becker, leader of the "Committee of Seven," whose task was to save important materials for Austria and to assist the politically persecuted. Fritz Molden and Ernst Lemberger narrowly escaped capture and managed to reach Switzerland. Their next task was to request restriction of Allied air raids on Austria to strictly military targets. This was of importance because very great damage to cultural installations and monuments was being caused by massive raids of the 15th US Air Force.

In September the Nazi leaders had still believed that the Viennese would stand their ground against the Red Army. That confidence was evaporating under the impact of constant air raids. The Nazi officials began to fear that the people would rise against them in revolt. "They would shoot us if they were armed!" one of them admitted frankly. One of his colleagues declared that he dared to enter his district only with pistol in hand for fear of being stoned by angry women. Another noted with marked resignation: "We don't have to wait for the Russians to arrive. The people will kill us even before they appear!"

A security report described the workers' districts in full ferment. Wherever Nazi functionaries showed up, they were greeted with a flood of abuse. One official cited a number of highly uncomplimentary expletives "even with regard to the person of our Führer," which that poor wretch apparently considered blasphemous. The Nazis were clearly scared of the working women of Vienna, who openly shouted at them: "Hang them all! The Nazi bandits are to blame for the death of so many men, women, and children!" When a Nazi officer tried to arrest a "Communist agitator" at a large bakery, women barred his way and helped the man to escape.

Desertion had increased to such an extent that it was estimated in March 1945 that 40,000 men were hiding in Vienna alone, mostly with forged identity papers. The city also had to harbor a growing number of refugees from Hungary, and all the hospitals were filled with wounded soldiers and civilians. More forced laborers—mainly Hungarian Jews—were transported to Austria to work on the defense line.

With its armies in retreat and its allies defecting, the Nazi regime still maintained its grip on the civilian population. The government agencies and the immense police apparatus were still functioning. The party members—about 500,000 persons—were urged to fight for survival and were told that defeat would mean utter annihilation.[2]

Meanwhile, the destruction of Austrian cities went on with the 15th US Air Force's intensified bombing. During the first months of 1945, Vienna suffered 51 air raids, in which the Opera, the Burgtheater, City Hall, Schönbrunn Castle, the Belvedere, the University, the former parliament building, and one museum were severely damaged. In all, 43 cultural institutions and 27 churches were hit. The Prater, an old amusement park, was in ruins. The Gestapo headquarters, where so many political prisoners had been tortured and killed, was completely destroyed. The destruction of the Opera on March 12, 1945, was a great blow to the Viennese. That attack was in all probability an error; it originally had been aimed at a chemical factory near Vienna, but was redirected toward the center because of heavy clouds. The bombers seem to have mistaken the building for a railroad station. To make the disaster worse, the firemen who were sent to combat the flames were foreign workers who were half-starved, did not understand German, and were somewhat less than enthusiastic in their efforts. The opera building burned for almost 24 hours, and thousands of citizens assembled to watch the flames. On that same day the German army carried out its last offensive action of World War II. Its goal was to dislodge the Russians in Hungary who had taken Budapest on February 12 and were preparing their advance toward the Austrian border.

[2] Nothing could be further from the truth; only a few prominent war criminals were executed by the Allies. The restored Austrian republic sentenced only 38 Nazis to death.

The offensive undertaken by SS General Sepp Dietrich's 6th Panzer Army was ill-conceived and ended in complete failure. After a few days of laborious advance through the mud and morass of central Hungary, the Russians under Marshal Feodor Ivanovich Tolbukhin pushed the Germans back south of Lake Balaton. Hitler was so angry about this defeat that he ordered four SS divisions stripped of their armbands because, he said, "the troops have not fought as the situation demanded." Dietrich, one of the Führer's old cronies, ignored the order. In fact, the SS troops had resisted with bravery, but were hopelessly outnumbered. Tolbukhin's 3rd Ukranian Front drove them irresistibly toward the Austrian border, while farther north Marshal Rodion Jakovlevich Malinowsky approached at a slower pace with his 2nd Ukranian Front.

Early spring in Vienna had an atmosphere of unreality. Baldur von Schirach assembled 16-year-old boys, drafted them into the *Volkssturm*, at a concert hall, and urged them to fight to the utmost. He had recently visited the Führer, who expected great things of those young men.[3] Mayor Blaschke, not to be outdone, proclaimed that "hunger, ruins, and ashes are the guarantees of our greatness." The food supply was constantly deteriorating; people began to trade all kinds of possessions for anything edible. Many Viennese were without electricity; public transportation became erratic. There were frequent air alarms, but some people were so busy foraging for food that they did not even care to take shelter. From March 12 until April 4 the U.S. Air Force operated daily over Austria; there was very little opposition from the Luftwaffe. All this did not prevent a certain deceptive mood of normalcy. On March 26 a soccer match in the suburb of Hütteldorf was watched by 8,000 fans. There were still occasional concerts; executions at the Vienna District Court went on with lugubrious

---

[3] After his release from Spandau prison in 1966, Schirach told a somewhat different story. He found the Führer at that last visit mentally and physically decrepit and enraged against the Viennese.

regularity. Military offenders were now handled by roving courts martial that operated with a minimum of formality and simply hanged convicted men from any convenient steel structure. Secretly, preparations were made to liquidate political prisoners. On March 28, Heinrich Himmler arrived in Vienna in an armored train and held a conference with the Austrian district leaders and several military commanders. The defeated units of General Dietrich were already streaming into Lower Austria and the Burgenland. The concentration of SS divisions made it clear that the Nazi leadership had decided to make a resolute stand in and around Vienna.

The Red Army crossed the Austrian-Hungarian border at Köszeg (Guens) on March 20. That area was defended by Hungarian troops and *Volkssturm* units with inadequate training and arms. They were no match for Tolbukhin's battle-hardened veterans. The Soviet Marshal viewed the Austrian plain and its alpine background from the *Rosaliengebirge*.[4] Since the days of Count Alexander Suvorov (1799), no Russian army had advanced so far to the West. In Vienna the sound of artillery became audible.

A few days earlier, the o 5 leadership had met with members of the military resistance that was directed by Karl Szokoll, the lone survivor of the July 20th putsch. He had been promoted to the rank of major and systematically established a new Resistance network within Army Command XVII. He and other officers surrounded themselves with fellow Austrians who could be relied upon to act when the time was ripe. It was clear that the critical moment was now rapidly approaching. In a number of military units the Resistance had established groups that were able to take command. The underground controlled a strong battery of howitzers, several infantry batallions, and about 2,000 other soldiers in various units. Furthermore, there existed a number of militant formations of armed civilians. There was also a strong Resistance team within the Vienna police force.

---

[4] The Rosalian Mountains near the border in the Burgenland.

One of the Austrian officers, First Lieutenant Wolfgang Igler, had learned from a German major that two additional SS divisions were being moved to Vienna. Clearly, there was no time to lose. Szokoll decided that contact with the Red Army had now become imperative. A detailed plan of insurrection was prepared. Its goal was to surrender the city to the Russians before it became a battlefield.

14
THE RUSSIANS ARE COMING!

On April 2, 1945, Easter Monday, Schirach had posters plastered all over Vienna, urging women and children to leave the city. He failed to advise them where to go, however. There was actually neither transportation nor fuel left to make a large-scale exodus possible. The last reports by Nazi functionaries speak of a rapidly deteriorating situation. "I have been deeply shaken by the lack of our leadership," wrote one of those officials. "If there is no quick change, Vienna will be taken by the Bolsheviks."

A few hours after his poster action, Schirach introduced his old friend, Colonel General of the Waffen SS Sepp Dietrich, as "Vienna's foremost defender." The city was declared a fortress and General Rudolf von Bünau was appointed commander of the defense zone. The general had placed Major Szokoll on his staff and unknowingly put him in a position to paralyze the German defense from within. Vienna was to be defended mainly by four SS divisions, with two more on the way from the Oder front. The rest were regular *Wehrmacht, Volkssturm,* and Hitler Youth. The two latter formations were concentrated in the western districts of Vienna, where no major activity was expected.

With the Soviet army only 35 miles from Vienna, Major Szokoll held an emergency meeting at his headquarters on the Stubenring, scene of the ill-fated July 20th plot. A sergeant, Ferdinand Käs, volunteered to undertake the risky mission to contact the Red Army. Chauffeured by Corporal Johann Reif, another member of the Resistance, Käs made his way through the German lines and reached a Soviet outpost at dawn on April 3. He was fortunate enough to encounter a Russian lieutenant who knew German and passed him on to 3rd Ukrainian Front headquarters at Hochwolkersdorf, 10 miles south of Wiener Neustadt. Brought before three Soviet generals and their staff, Käs outlined Szokoll's plan to deliver the city to the Russians without further fighting. He explained that the Resistance could help the Soviet troops to enter Vienna from the weakly defended western suburbs.

Understandably, the Russian officers were at first suspicious. But when Käs pointed out the German positions on a map and these were found to tally with their own reports, they agreed to inform the High Command in Moscow. On the next morning, cooperation between o 5 and the Soviet army was agreed upon. The Allies were requested to stop bombing Vienna and Lower Austria from the air. Käs and Reif now returned to Vienna; ironically, they got a lift from an official of the Nazi Party. On that same day, the Russians penetrated the German positions between Wiener Neustadt and Baden and began an outflanking movement through the Vienna Woods.

On that dramatic April 5, 1945, unknown to both the German High Command and the o 5 leadership, another meeting took place at Soviet headquarters in Hochwolkersdorf. An elderly man from nearby Gloggnitz had appeared to complain about the behavior of some Russian soldiers. He was Dr. Karl Renner, former chancellor and president of parliament in the first Austrian Republic. Renner was 74 years old and had lived in retirement during the last seven years. He had no political ambitions, but merely hoped that his former high office would at least enable him to be listened to. He could not expect great sympathy from the Communists. As a moderate Social Democrat he had been called a "traitor to Socialism" by Lenin, long since deified in the Soviet Union.

To his surprise, Renner was treated very gently by the Russians, who quickly decided that he could be very useful to them. After all, a provisional Austrian government was a necessity, and an old, respected politician like Renner seemed just the right person to be its head. When he left Soviet headquarters, he had agreed to convoke parliament, to appoint a provisional cabinet, and to prepare elections. This provisional Austrian government did not come into existence until three weeks later, but Renner's agreement with the Soviets at Hochwolkersdorf was the initial step for the rebirth of the Austrian Republic.

At noon of April 5, Major Szokoll was informed by Käs that the Russians were now advancing in a northwesterly direction. When they reached the outskirts of the city, they were to fire a red light signal and the Resistance would reply with a green flare. The last preparations were now made for the final uprising in Vienna.

The revolt was to start on Friday, April 6, at 8 P.M. with the construction of barricades and active help for the advancing Soviet troops. Austrian units under Major Karl Biedermann were to occupy railroad stations and road junctions. Baldur von Schirach and General von Bünau were to be arrested and forced to issue an order declaring Vienna an open city and announcing an immediate cease-fire. Such an apparently legal order undoubtedly would be obeyed by all commanders. Simultaneously, all broadcasting stations would be occupied, and at 11:30 P.M. Major Szokoll, the new commander of the city, would surrender Vienna to the Russians and order the Waffen SS divisions to withdraw.

Szokoll's plan would have succeeded but for an unexpected betrayal. One of Major Biedermann's junior officers, Lieutenant

Walter Hanslik, became suspicious of the intended troop movements. The lieutenant, a convinced National Socialist, warned General von Bünau. Major Biedermann was ordered to report to headquarters. He obeyed, although he must have guessed that his situation was becoming very critical. Perhaps he feared that an attempt to escape would endanger the conspiracy. At headquarters Biedermann was arrested, questioned for many hours, and finally tortured. In the early morning hours of April 6 he broke down and divulged the names of his fellow plotters. Thereupon Major Neumann, Bünau's Chief of Staff, ordered an SS unit to seize Army Command XVII headquarters. Szokoll happened to be absent, but his closest collaborators, Captain Alfred Huth and First Lieutenant Rudolf Raschke, were arrested. An alert secretary managed to warn Major Szokoll by phone and burned some highly compromising documents literally under the eyes of the SS. But the original plan for the uprising was now doomed to failure. The SS commandeered all motor vehicles that were to have been used by the insurgents. The army units which Szokoll planned to use against the SS remained for a great part inactive. Szokoll, Käs, and the civilian leadership of o 5 were not caught and continued their actions, but the decisive blow against the German High Command had miscarried.

Biedermann, Huth, and Raschke were court-martialed, driven to a public square on the far side of the Danube, and hanged from lampposts that served as gallows. Alfred Huth was stabbed in the face with a bayonet before being executed. The corpses were left hanging for days.

Although the uprising had been thwarted, fear and confusion began to spread among the city's defenders. General von Bünau had been badly shaken by the realization that his own officers had intended to arrest him. On the other hand, the SS—never on the best of terms with the army—suspected that his whole staff had been infiltrated by the Resistance. When von Bünau reported to Berlin that his men were attacked by partisans, Hitler wired furiously: "Proceed against the rebels in Vienna with most brutal measures."

And now, in all that general confusion, came the blow of the Russian offensive. The first thrust came predictably in the south, where the Germans feverishly erected barricades against the Soviet tanks. On April 7 part of the city was already within range of the Russian artillery. Then, suddenly and unexpectedly, a second assault hit the western outskirts. Here the defense simply disintegrated. The *Volkssturm* men offered hardly any resistance; most of them changed back to civilian status, abandoning their weapons. They had no desire to fight for Hitler. Numerous volunteers helped Soviet units to circumvent German positions, and Marshal Tolbukhin's broadcast appeal for aid for his troops found ready listeners. White and red-white-red flags appeared everywhere. In the workers' districts the population turned against the German soldiers. Women with babies in their arms shouted at them to go home. Snipers fired at the bewildered Germans from roofs and windows. General Dietrich's Chief of Staff reported that his troops were under fire not from Russians but from Austrian partisans. On April 8 the Red Army reached the *Gürtel* of Vienna, the belt that encircles the 10 inner districts of the city. Here they came to a temporary halt. A large number of buildings stood in flames. In complete disregard of his duties, Mayor Hanns Blaschke ordered the fire brigades to leave the city. About 3,800 men and 627 motor vehicles were sent to Upper Austria, while behind them fires lit up the night sky. The Russians were using their fighter bombers as flying artillery. The Luftwaffe in the eastern part of Austria was down to about 120 aircraft. The Americans had stopped their raids so as not to endanger their Russian allies. The retreating Germans destroyed gas works and power stations.

The German forces in Austria suddenly got a new commanding officer, Colonel General Lothar Rendulic, until recently in command of the 20th Mountain Army in northern Norway. Rendulic, an Austrian Nazi of long standing, arrived in Vienna on April 8 and, being a rational man, he saw immediately that the battle was lost. He later claimed that he disregarded Hitler's order to defend Vienna to the last. Nevertheless, the struggle went on for five more days.

Another late arrival was SS Colonel Otto Skorzeny, Hitler's expert for daredevil commando actions. After driving around in the almost deserted city, he came to the same conclusion as Rendulic. He frankly told Bünau and Schirach that chaos reigned on the roads leading to the West and that the city was virtually lost. Schirach contradicted him with some bravado but seems to have had second thoughts by the next morning. When the Resistance cut the electric current to his air raid shelter at the Hofburg, the former imperial palace in the center of Vienna, he lost his nerve. Forgetting all his poems that praised heroism and self-sacrifice, Schirach fled from Vienna, made his way to the Tyrol, tried to assume a false identity, and finally surrendered to the Americans. He was tried as a major war criminal in Nuremberg, sentenced to 20 years in jail, and released from Spandau Prison in 1966. In his memoirs he later sought to defend his actions and play down the extent of his guilt. Schirach died in 1974.

His deputy, Karl Scharizer, showed more courage. He joined the *Volkssturm* and was taken prisoner by the Russians. Mayor Blaschke had no stomach for heroics. After a half-hearted attempt to negotiate with the Resistance, he hastily left the city. His order to withdraw the fire brigades and their equipment was to cause widespread damage and suffering to the Viennese.[1] Another Nazi leader, Karl Mayerzett, fled to Upper Austria and was promptly executed for desertion by the fanatical district leader Eigruber. Even Skorzeny, who was certainly no coward, did not join the fighting. He wired the Führer that Vienna was defenseless and left.

From April 9 on, conditions in Vienna turned completely chaotic. Dietrich's SS troops found themselves totally isolated among a

---

[1] A number of fires were caused by looters and young Nazi desperadoes known as the "werewolves."

hostile population. Most other units had surrendered, shed their uniforms, or simply melted away. Some soldiers who had changed to civilian attire but had forgotten to remove their dog tags were shot by the Russians, who mistook them for disguised Nazi partisans.

The Resistance had recovered from its initial setback and made the Auersperg Palace in the center of Vienna its new headquarters. What remained of the o 5 leadership assembled in that building. One member of the military resistance got hold of the German defense plan of the inner city. Major Szokoll decided to take it personally to the Russian High Command. This time he was successful.

The first Russian crack units that advanced into the center were quite friendly toward the population. On Schwarzenberg Square a good-natured army cook peacefully distributed food among children. Unfortunately, those who arrived later were far less disciplined, and during the following days rape and looting were common. As usual, many perfectly innocent people became the victims. A tragic example is the case of Lieutenant Colonel Georg Bartl, formerly Schuschnigg's aide-de-camp. After long imprisonment at Mauthausen he lived in retirement near Klosterneuburg. He welcomed the Russians as liberators, but a horde of drunken soldiers raped his wife and four other women who had taken refuge in his house. On the morning after that outrage, Bartl shot the five women and finally himself.

However, it would not be fair to blame all the violence of those days on the Russians. The foreign slave laborers whom the Nazis had dragged to Austria from all parts of Europe now took the opportunity to get even with their oppressors. Among the looters were also quite a number of Viennese. It was easy to rob storehouses and shops during the general chaos. The large customhouse was plundered during a raid by low-flying Soviet planes. When it was over, the dead and the wounded lay among heaps of stolen shoes and textiles. A number of wine cellars were broken into by Russians as well as Austrian civilians, with predictable results. In

some districts, persons with and without uniform established themselves as an emergency police force. As in 1938, goods were confiscated, neighbors expelled, and many old accounts settled.

The most appalling fate befell a large number of political
prisoners who were held at the Vienna county court. Some of those
men—among them a few politicians—were released, but the others
were marched in chains to the prison at Stein, Lower Austria. This
installation had already witnessed a frightful massacre on April 6.
The governor, Franz Kodré,[2] intended to release his prisoners.
However, the SS intervened, murdered 368 inmates, and executed
the governor and three of his aides. When the unfortunate prisoners from Vienna arrived, they were at first put into prison cells. On
April 14, when the struggle for Vienna had already ended, the
SS carried out their second massacre. Only a very few managed
to escape.[3]

In Vienna, April 10 was a day of intense fighting. Using their
feared rocket launchers, *"Stalinorgeln"* (Stalin organs), the Soviets
reached the Ring, the broad treelined boulevard that encircles the
inner city. The already damaged Burgtheater was burning fiercely.
Nearby, City Hall with its neo-Gothic tower stood empty, the
civil servants having all fled. The Germans were pushed back to
the Danube Canal, which flows west of the river and borders the
city center. While retreating they blew up the bridges, leaving
many of their wounded behind them. Their artillery now fired on
the inner city and set the roof of St. Stephen's cathedral ablaze.
Eventually, the whole choir collapsed and caused grave damage to
the inside of the great dome.[4]

The grim struggle went on in the districts between the Canal
and the river. The SS fought with its usual ferocity. A few hours
before their final retreat they executed nine Jews who had been

[2] He was the brother of Colonel Heinrich Kodré.
[3] One of the survivors, Father Ignaz Kühmayer, a member of the Scholz group,
later narrated his experiences (see Bibliography).
[4] The damage could have even been greater had not a German artillery officer,
Captain Gerhard Klinkicht, refused to fire his battery on the church. He was
later decorated by the Austrian government.

hiding during the whole occupation and were accidentally detected by soldiers. Among those victims was an 82-year-old woman. Armed Russian trawlers appeared on the Danube, landing commandos and pouring their fire on the Germans.

To General Rendulic, the final phase of the fighting in Vienna was merely a delaying action. On April 13 the two northern bridges over the Danube were blown up, and this left only the Reichsbrücke as the last escape route. When the last Germans had retreated over that bridge, a demolition party approached. However, the Austrian soldiers who guarded the structure were o 5 men, and they suddenly opened fire on the Germans and drove them off. What was left of the German army retreated on both river banks in the direction of Tulln. General Rendulic, fearing complete encirclement, was eager to extricate his tired units. His worries were justified, for Marshal Malinowsky's 2nd Ukrainian Front had crossed the Danube and was pressing its attack on the northern bank of the river.

The city was now in Russian hands, and the Soviet press expanded lyrically on the hometown of Beethoven and Schubert. A popular photo of those days shows Russian soldiers decorating the monument of Johann Strauss, the Waltz King.

15
THE ALPINE REDOUBT

In July 1944 the district leader of Tyrol, Franz Hofer, sent a memorandum to Hitler that urged the building of a defense system reaching from the Bavarian Alps to Lake Garda. A more detailed plan followed in November. In the east the fortress area was to run from Steyr to the river Drau. The western approaches would be guarded by the Arlberg, while the southern line would be on Italian territory, partly following the old Austrian front line of World War I. In the north the defenses were to be built along the previous Austro-German border. The fortified area was to form a rectangle that included the whole southern part of Austria and Italian South Tyrol. An additional defense line, the *Voralpenstellung*, was to protect the industrial cities of Linz and Steyr in the north. Hitler accepted Hofer's plan, but only on April 11, with Germany already in a state of collapse, was he called to Berlin for a conference on the project. When the order to build the alpine redoubt was finally given on April 28, the war was virtually over.

The great stronghold was never built, although three generals were appointed to command it.

In the meantime, the Allies had gotten wind of the project and took it very seriously. The idea that the Nazis would make a last-ditch stand in the Alps seemed not illogical. General Eisenhower decided to swing his 6th Army group into Western Austria; that move would prevent the building of Hitler's "national redoubt." Eisenhower planned to occupy the major mountain passes in the north and then push forward towards the Italian border. The German forces would be crushed between a three-pronged drive from Bavaria—north and west—and from Italy (see maps).

In the meantime, events on the Italian front took a decisive turn. Here 27 German divisions opposed a weaker Allied force, but their air support was almost gone, and because of Hitler's obstinacy they occupied a vulnerable position south of the river Po. One of the German commanders, SS General Karl Wolff, was secretly in contact with the Allies to negotiate a local surrender. However, these contacts brought no results, and on April 9 the Allied offensive started. After 11 days of fighting, the German front in the Adriatic sector collapsed and General Heinrich von Vietinghoff ordered a general retreat. This "mobile strategy" quickly turned into a rout which was aggravated by an Italian partisan uprising. During the last days of April, the German forces in Italy were overcome by total disaster. Under those circumstances, Vietinghoff did the only rational thing: he surrendered his army unconditionally at Caserta on April 29. Vietinghoff was perfectly aware of the fact that a prolonged defense in the Alps was simply not feasible. There were neither sufficient troops nor enough materiel and fuel available. Allied troops had already crossed the river Adige and were advancing toward Austria's southern border. There was mounting apprehension that the whole south of Austria would now be turned into a battlefield. Considering the mentality of the Nazi leaders, it seemed possible that they would try to make their last stand in the alpine region in spite of the hopeless military situation. For the inhabitants of the hypothetical stronghold—almost all Austrians—the consequences would be fatal. The far superior Allied air force could destroy the whole area in a matter of days. Many Austrians who had so far remained passive felt that the time had come to take action.

The Tyrolean Resistance was well entrenched in and around Innsbruck, especially among several army units. Unbeknownst to the Nazis, one mountain battalion was commanded by a Resistance man, Major Werner Heine. Plans for an uprising were in the making, but clearly it could only succeed when Allied troops were near enough to intervene.

Among the German diehards, illusions about a sudden reversal of alliances persisted. They hoped that the United States and Britain would accept them as allies against the Soviet Union. Up to the very end, such rumors were systematically circulated.

The Resistance was better informed, since the o 5 organization maintained an office in Zurich. The decision to divide Austria and Germany into military zones had been made long ago. No Allied power was willing to deal with Nazi functionaries. Austria had to rid itself of the still remaining power structure of the Third Reich.

On April 13, the day Vienna fell to the Russians, the underground held a secret meeting in Innsbruck. Karl Gruber, a seasoned anti-Nazi activist, was appointed commander. Jörg Sackenheim, who maintained contacts with the Ötztal partisans, was to coordinate all civilian resistance groups. Communications were in the hands of Karl Hirnschrott, a capable expert who operated from the Innsbruck telephone center. A secret radio transmitter had been installed weeks before by American paratroopers on the Kemateralm, about 5,300 feet above sea level, in the area commanded by Major Heine.

A premature action of the underground caused a serious setback. On April 20, Hitler's birthday, Austrian flags and anti-Nazi leaflets appeared in Innsbruck. The still active Gestapo countered with a wave of arrests and discovered the secret radio transmitter. Two

American officers were captured and Major Heine had a narrow escape. General Valentin Feuerstein, Heine's superior, who was suspected of sympathizing with the Resistance, was deposed and replaced by a fervent Nazi, General Johannes Böhaimb.

At that point neither the Resistance fighters nor their pursuers knew about the secret negotiations between the Allies and the German high command in Italy. District leader Hofer declared that he would fight to the last. And then a flood of events followed. The German army in Italy surrendered, Hitler committed suicide, and Mussolini was caught and executed. And while district leader Hofer in a windy broadcast urged his countrymen to continue fighting, the 7th US Army started moving from the north. The American offensive aimed at the Fernpass in northern Tyrol, while further to the west the 1st French Army began to attack Vorarlberg.

On April 30, Innsbruck was filled with rumors about an American breakthrough. There was a brief panic among the local Nazis, but then it became known that the American troops who were advancing in a heavy snowstorm had not yet traversed the mountain passes.

On May 2 the revolt erupted. One Resistance group occupied the Conrad barracks in Innsbruck, while a second, commanded by Sackenheim, carried out a surprise attack against SS headquarters. A third detachment captured the police barracks. General Böhaimb was peacefully dining at the Hotel Mariabrunn, when suddenly Major Heine appeared with 20 insurgents and placed him under arrest.

The next hours were chaotic. The Resistance presented Hofer with an ultimatum to surrender. The wily *Gauleiter* prevaricated, finally fled Innsbruck, and alarmed the SS. A regular battle took place in the center of the city. The SS troopers succeeded in liberating General Böhaimb, but then they were driven from the city by the insurgents, who were now in possession of machine guns and even some artillery. One of the leaders of the underground, Franz Mair, fell right in front of the Landhaus, but by 5 P.M. the SS was forced

5th US Army, which was advancing from the Italian front. The rapid progress of Patton's troops from the north had taken everybody by surprise. Consequently, the first American units were in no way prepared to deal with the Austrians. It was weeks before a uniform military government could be established. In Upper Austria the situation looked very serious because district leader August Eigruber, a mindless fanatic, announced his willingness to fight to the last man. While the Viennese held their first May Day parade, the Nazi terror in Upper Austria still claimed its victims. On May 1 Eigruber had another 13 freedom fighters executed. Fortunately, some of the German generals were far less sanguine, and when American troops advanced on Linz, they simply gave up.

In the nearby concentration camp of Mauthausen,[2] a military Resistance group had existed for months. On May 4 most of the SS guards fled; the underground took over and held the camp until the Americans arrived. The soldiers were horrified by the conditions they found in the camp. Everywhere there were traces of seven years of systematic mistreatment and extermination. During that period about 120,000 persons, inmates from all over Europe, had died there. The most terrible memento was the so-called "staircase of death" and the "ramp of the parachutists," where innumerable prisoners had been pushed into a stone quarry to their death. The survivors were pitiful, emaciated human beings, many of them maimed for life.

A drama of a very different kind occurred in the salt mines of the Salzkammergut region in Upper Austria. The Germans employed a labyrinth of disused underground passages for the storage of art treasures looted from all parts of occupied Europe. Among other works, that hoard contained the famous Ghent Triptych painted by Hubert and Jan van Eyck, 15 paintings taken from

---

[2] Later on Mauthausen became a memorial shrine which contains monuments honoring the victims of many nations. A camp museum traces the history of this place of horror and constitutes an impressive reminder of man's inhumanity to man.

the Paris Rothschild collection, and a number of other priceless works of Dutch, Flemish, and French masters.[3] When district leader Eigruber realized that the fate of the Third Reich was sealed, he decided to blow up the whole complex of underground mine-shafts and galleries with all its hidden treasure. He ordered an explosive expert to place bomb charges within the mine, and this insane act of destruction would have been carried out had not a Resistance group gotten wind of his plan. Eigruber's bombardier was promptly captured and the explosive charges were removed. A second attempt was frustrated by Resistance fighters, who blocked all entrances to the mine. Simultaneously, a message concerning Eigruber's mad project reached the Americans. On May 8 a U.S. advance party reached the salt mine and secured its valuable store of masterworks. Eigruber fled, but was arrested by the American Military Police and was later executed as a war criminal.

During the last weeks of the war, National Socialist officials and various satellite agencies kept pouring into the alpine area. The most prominent arrival was the notorious police chief Ernst Kalten-brunner, who suddenly recalled his Austrian origins and even attempted to form a new Austrian government. Of course, he found no support for this preposterous idea, for it was obvious that Kaltenbrunner ranked high on the Allied list of war criminals. Deserted by all his followers, the disappointed security chief sought refuge in a lonely cabin in a remote alpine region. Undoubtedly he hoped to disappear for a period of time and to leave secretly when the coast seemed clear. However, a Resistance fighter named Sepp Plieseis, who had long been active in that area, had watched Kaltenbrunner's movements and informed the US Military Police. Kaltenbrunner was arrested, tried at Nuremberg before the Allied tribunal, and hanged on October 16, 1946. He was one of the most sinister figures to have arisen from the Nazi movement in Austria.

[3] Among many other masterworks, the mine contained paintings by Vermeer, Watteau, and Fragonard. Many art treasures from Viennese museums were also stored at the same location.

The final phase of the war in Salzburg and Upper Austria ended with little bloodshed. Allied paratroopers, among them several Austrians, including Albrecht Gaiswinkler,[4] played a decisive part in checkmating the Nazis. In Salzburg the German town commander offered only token resistance. In the scenic resort area around Bad Aussee, British paratroopers, aided by the underground, controlled a region that was swarming with German troops.

The situation was different in Lower Styria and Carinthia, where chaos threatened and hostilities persisted even after the German surrender. On May 7, 1945 at Reims, General Alfred Jodl signed the historic document which ordered the unconditional surrender of all German troops. Hostilities were to cease at noon on May 9, but in some parts of Austria World War II was still going on. At Yalta in February 1945, demarcation lines had been specified. When this became clear to the Germans and their satellites, whose troops were retreating from Yugoslavia, a desperate scramble began to avoid capture by Soviet troops. In many cases the Germans became the victims of their own propaganda, which had made them believe that the US and Britain would end up fighting the Russians with German help. When all this turned out to be nothing more than wishful thinking, panic set in. Hundreds of thousands of Germans and their auxiliaries—mainly dissident Croatians and Russians—tried hastily to reach the British demarcation line. This led to enormous confusion and sometimes to prolonged fighting, for several SS units refused to surrender and went on a mad rampage. Atrocious scenes took place at the small town of Hartberg in Styria, where mass executions and imprisonment of Austrian patriots had occurred a few days prior to the German surrender. When the SS was finally forced to leave, they dragged 26 men and 3 women from the city jail and slaughtered them on their retreat. In Donawitz the SS attempted to destroy the important steel works, but the underground managed to occupy them before any explo-

---

[4] Albrecht Gaiswinkler, a veteran of the Spanish civil war, was imprisoned by the Gemans but managed to escape and joined the Allied Forces. Trained as a paratrooper he became a leading figure in the alpine resistance.

sives could be detonated. The long-smoldering partisan war between the Nazis and the Resistance continued in that region for
several days after the German capitulation. Tragically, one of the
leaders of the Styrian Resistance, Franz Lindmoser, lost his life
on the day after the cease-fire during a skirmish with retreating
SS troops.

In Graz, the capital of Styria, once a Nazi stronghold, the end
came peaceably. The well-organized underground movement designated one of its leaders, the Socialist Reinhard Machold, for the
position of provincial governor. Despite the presence of SS units,
Machold simply went to government headquarters, the Landhaus,
and demanded that all executive powers be transferred to him. The
National Socialists withdrew without offering any resistance. When
Soviet troops occupied Graz 12 hours later, they were welcomed
by the new government. The Russian presence in Graz was only
temporary, however, for the city was later incorporated into the
British zone of occupation.

In Carinthia conditions were extremely complicated. All roads
were blocked by fleeing German columns that did not wish to
surrender to the Red Army and their Yugoslav and Bulgarian
auxiliaries. Along those roads abandoned vehicles and arms marked
the German retreat. The collapse of the German authorities became apparent on May 4, and on the next day the Resistance took
the risky step of confronting the Nazi district leader, Friedrich
Rainer, with its demands. Four members of the underground nego-
tiated with Rainer, who still held power enough to order their
arrest and execution. These strange parleys went on for four days.
In the meantime the British were slowly advancing from Italy and
reached the Austrian border at Tarvis on May 7. In the southeastern corner of Carinthia, Bulgarian and Yugoslav troops blocked
the retreating Germans at the river Drau. After many complications, Rainer finally resigned. He probably feared that the Yugoslavs, who entered Klagenfurt only a few hours after the British,
would simply hang him. The arrival of Tito's partisan army, which
claimed parts of Carinthia by right of conquest, had not been

expected. However, Carinthia belonged to the British zone of occupation, and the Yugoslavs eventually were persuaded to leave.

Another complication arose from the surrender to the British army of about 30,000 Cossacks who had fought on the German side. According to the Yalta agreement, POWs had to be returned to their country of origin. Consequently, these prisoners had to be extradited to the USSR. A number of them committed suicide by drowning themselves in the river Mur at the Russian demarcation line.

In Lower Austria no major military action took place after the fall of Vienna. The Russians did not pursue their offensive. The German troops under General Rendulic that were still in the area eventually surrendered to the Americans.[5]

When the shooting finally stopped, all of Austria was under occupation, although many changes in the zonal demarcation lines were still to come. Renner's government had not yet been recognized by the West and functioned only with very limited authority in the Soviet zone. In the middle of widespread devastation and confusion, the Austrians were now faced with the task of rebuilding their country.

---

[5] About a half-million German soldiers, most of them hastily crossing the river Enns, eventually became POWs in American hands. Most of these troops originally had confronted the Soviet armies.

16
THE AFTERMATH

The end of the war and the total collapse of Hitler's Thousand-Year Reich was greeted by most Austrians with a sigh of relief. Aside from a small number of diehard fanatics, no one regretted that World War II had finally come to an end after 5½ years of bloodshed and unparalleled destruction. The situation was quite different from World War I, during which the civilian population had suffered deprivations but neither casualties nor damage from air attacks and street fighting.

The Austrian statistics on seven years of German occupation looked particularly grim regarding military and civilian loss of life:

170,800 Austrians killed in battle
 76,200 missing
 24,300 civilian casualties
 65,500 Austrian Jews killed by the Nazis
 32,600 Austrians dead in Nazi camps or prisons
  2,700 Austrians executed
————
372,100

Austria had lost 5.8% of its population as a direct result of the war and the German occupation. Most of those who had welcomed the invasion of 1938 now had good reason to mourn; few families had survived the war without the loss of relatives. But those figures did not tell the full story. The number of those whose health had permanently suffered from injuries, ill-treatment, and privations cannot be established. At the end of the war about 750,000 Austrian soldiers had become POWs. Those captured during the last weeks by the Western Allies were soon released and those detained in Britain, France, or the US followed shortly thereafter. The Soviet Union began to repatriate Austrian prisoners only in September 1947, and it took many years until the last ones returned.

A permanent loss were the thousands of scientists, writers, composers, and other intellectuals who had emigrated after the *Anschluss*. Only a small number of them returned to their homeland. The cultural life of Austria never completely recovered from that bloodletting.[1]

Among the liberated countries of Europe, Austria found itself in a strange and singular position. In Holland, Belgium, and Norway the legal government had been in exile and simply returned when the war was over. In Denmark it had not even left the country. In France and Yugoslavia the Resistance had produced leaders who could provide guidance for their nations. Unfortunately, the Austrian opposition to Hitler had many brave members but no great personalities of the caliber of Charles de Gaulle or Marshal Tito. In fact, most Resistance leaders were little known to the public. Even today, the names of some deserving leaders of the wartime opposition are relatively unknown to their countrymen. Perhaps this was because many of the surviving Austrian Resistance fighters had no political ambition. When the Nazis were finally defeated, they just faded back into private life. The o 5 organization soon ceased to exist. People returned to their old political parties and,

[1] A large number of famous Austrians, including Sigmund Freud, Franz Werfel, Stefan Zweig, Josef Roth, Hermann Broch, Arnold Schönberg, Max Reinhardt, Felix Salten, and Alfred Polgar, died in exile.

once the mutual enemy was gone, the wartime spirit of solidarity and sacrifice receded. The same phenomenon occurred in other formerly occupied countries. However, in France or Holland the Resistance had acquired a degree of glory, even a certain mystique, which survived. Furthermore, the Allies quite correctly considered the Resistance fighters of those countries as their brothers-in-arms. In Austria the attitude of the occupying powers varied according to political considerations. Major Szokoll, the leader of the Vienna military underground, was even arrested by the Russians on charges of being a Western spy, and spent several months in a prison camp. On the other hand, some extremely dubious characters were appointed to high offices in the police force on their claim that they were Communist Resistance fighters. The American, British, and French military authorities were often uninformed about the internal situation in Austria and found it difficult to distinguish between "good" and "bad" Austrians. Even among the Western powers a uniform approach to the Austrian problem was lacking. The first proclamation of Field Marshal Harold Alexander, for instance, said bluntly that the Allies had entered Austria as conquerors. By contrast, the French declared that they were coming as liberators and placed signs at the border designating Austria as friendly territory. The military authorities sometimes showed an amazing ignorance concerning the country they occupied.[2] Many people who had been opposed to the Nazis complained that they were being ignored and became embittered.

In Vienna, conditions during the first weeks after the German retreat remained chaotic. Renner's provisional government, consisting of 30 Ministers and State Secretaries, had little authority; at first it did not even possess an armed security force. A great number of crimes were committed; many persons used the general confusion to settle old accounts. As in 1938, murders occurred, houses were confiscated, and stores were looted. Rape was so com-

[2] The 42nd U.S. Infantry Division (the so-called Rainbow Division) proudly announced that it was entering "Tyrol, the land of Wilhelm Tell."

mon that illegal abortions during summer and fall 1945 were silently approved by the government. Conditions in Upper and Lower Austria were also precarious. Bands of marauders attacked villages and pillaged lonely farms.

In June 1945 the first British and American officers appeared in Vienna, but the division of the city into four occupation zones was not carried out until September 1. In the West of Austria, which was under American and French occupation, recovery proceeded at a faster pace. Damage due to air raids and artillery action was widespread all over the country. Some smaller towns were partly in ruins. Of the 4,200 buildings in the industrial center of Wiener Neustadt, 1,060 were completely destroyed, and of the remaining 3,140 only 18 escaped damage. In Vienna 193,000 homes, a large number of public buildings, and most bridges had fallen victim to American bombs and Russian and German shells and mines. The famous Ringstrasse was now a sorry sight, with many of its monumental buildings turned into blackened ruins. It took ten years to rebuild the Opera House and the Burgtheater. Vienna's oldest landmark, St. Stephen's cathedral, had been severely damaged by artillery fire and was not fully restored until 1952. Of the provincial capitals, Innsbruck had undergone the greatest devastation, with 53.6% of its buildings destroyed or damaged.

The slow consolidation of the Second Austrian Republic, which had its full sovereignty restored by the State Treaty of 1955, is not within the scope of this book. Austria long ago ceased to be Europe's problem child. However, a few words must be said concerning the changes that the years of war and oppression brought about in the thinking of the Austrians.

The First Republic was a product of World War I and the subsequent Treaty of Saint-Germain. At that time the idea that Austria was merely a construction dictated by political necessities was quite common. Confidence in the future and a firm resolve to maintain an independent state was at first lacking and only grew very slowly. All these doubts and uncertainties were revived by the great economic crisis of the 1930s. The Nazis very cleverly used the opportunity to convince many young people that fusion with the Reich would mean a prosperous future.

To both Catholics and Socialists, who constituted the great majority of the population, the Nazi ideology was anathema. However, certain pan-German tendencies were not completely foreign to them. In 1918 the Socialists had even favored *Anschluss*—of course, with a Socialist Germany. The Catholic politicians of the 1930s—men like Dollfuss and Schuschnigg—never preached hostility against the Reich; they merely rejected National Socialism and its pagan, anti-Christian, Prussian ideology. They proclaimed that Austrian patriots were actually the better Germans. They saw an independent, Catholic Austria as representative of true German and European civilization.[3] The German occupation of 1938 put an end to all those discussions. To Hitler the mere existence of Austria—even as a district of the Reich—was heresy. Even its name and its specific civilization had to disappear. As so often in history, it was exactly that attitude that led to a reversal. When the Austrians had lost every shred of liberty and independence, they remembered their heritage and their past. It was a painful lesson, but they learned it.

It is correct to say that a large percentage of the population only turned against the Nazis when it became clear that they were losing the war. Even then many remained inactive, and restricted their opposition to cautious grumbling, listening to foreign broadcasts, and dealing on the black market. The real Resistance always remained relatively small, and because the Nazis intensely persecuted it, it was decimated again and again. About 35,000 Austrians paid with their lives for their anti-Nazi activities. No really reliable data exist about the number of persons who were temporarily or permanently imprisoned because of political activities during

---

[3] Austrians talk of "German culture" in the same sense as Americans and Englishmen speak of Anglo-Saxon civilization. This has no political implications; however, many Austrians considered their country the sanctuary of German culture when the Reich began to sink into barbarism.

those years. Those who were released after a few years in a prison or concentration camp were often in such bad physical condition or so intimidated that they were lost to the movement of liberation. The numbers of those who subsequently died of injuries or diseases deriving from their imprisonment has never been determined. A greater number survived but never fully recovered their health. To the minor victims of National Socialism must also be added the many thousands who lost their jobs because they were known to be "politically unreliable." All this created an atmosphere of fear and intimidation which is hard for persons who have never lived under a similar reign of terror to imagine.

Until the last months of the war, the Resistance lacked inner cohesion and organized leadership. Cooperation with the Allies remained tenuous to the very last. The Resistance never established the close contacts with Allied intelligence that did serious damage to the German war machine in Denmark and Norway. This was partly because no effective Austrian organization existed in London. Only in the very last phase of the war did the o 5 organization manage to build valuable contacts with the Allies, particularly with the French.

The history of the Austrian Resistance remained for a very long time almost unknown. It is certainly a tragic story, because so many of its efforts were futile despite great human sacrifice and suffering. Many details did not become known until long after the war. To the Allies, the efforts of Austrian freedom fighters were only minor actions that did not greatly influence the course of the war. Consequently they remained almost unreported, and the Austrians themselves were rather reticent about them in the first years following World War II. This was the period of the Cold War, when Austria was still divided into occupation zones and faced an uncertain future. In the Russian zone any activity which could be described as pro-Western was supect, while the Americans did not look kindly upon real or supposed Communists. Among the population itself, the attitudes toward people who had aided the Russians was often downright hostile. The methods of Soviet occupation had caused widespread resentment. When the fiancée of Captain Huth[4] talked to journalists in 1955, she asked that her name be withheld; she feared difficulties with her neighbors, who would not understand how a German officer could have cooperated with the Russians. Of course, former Nazis considered their old opponents as outright traitors and "glorified snipers" who had stabbed Germany in the back.

Although National Socialism disappeared from the political scene in 1945, its vestiges persisted for a long time. Even 30 years after the end of World War II, the subject of the Resistance still evokes passionate debate. The Austrians have learned to live and work together peacefully, but among the older generation the past is still an agonizing subject and a source of sometimes acrimonious discussion.

Characteristically, there was far less bitterness toward the "enemy." Even while the war was still being fought, the average Austrian felt very little hostility toward the Americans, British, and French, although these nations had already been on the opposing side during World War I. There was far greater animosity toward the Italians, the traditional foes of Austria, who at least temporarily appeared as Germany's allies. When Italy changed sides in 1943, the general Austrian attitude was: "I told you so." Nazi propaganda was fairly successful against Russia, partly because many Austrians, as a result of experiences during the campaign in the East, were fully aware of the German atrocities and were fearful of retaliation. The ill-treatment and starvation to which Russian POWs and forced laborers had been subjected was common knowledge. When 700 Soviet prisoners escaped from Mauthausen in February 1945, 683 were killed during an organized manhunt. That the Red Army would be a vengeful conqueror was not difficult to foresee. By that time, far too many had become accomplices of Hitler's nationalistic and racist policies. There was no road back! It has always been the strategy of totalitarian gov-

---

[4] Huth was executed in April 1945 by the Germans for military conspiracy.

ernment to involve a great number of citizens in its crimes. Once tainted with the common guilt, the culprits could be trusted to fight well for self-preservation. However, in the end that policy was to fail, as the events during the Russian offensive against Vienna proved. Eventually, only the SS put up a real fight; the average Austrian soldier was not willing to sacrifice his life for a lost cause.

Some historians believe that the men who served in the SS and the Gestapo were a species apart, a sort of pathological savage. Undoubtedly, these organizations contained a goodly number of sadists, homicidal maniacs, and other deviates. However, the majority seem to have been relatively normal young men, mostly of a lower middle-class background. They were the product of an indoctrination so intense that the traditional principles of good and evil had lost all meaning. Every aspect of their service was strictly regulated, and the pressures of war, constant bullying by superiors, and a general atmosphere of brutality did the rest. The long duration of the war and the systematic hatemongering by press and radio dehumanized many persons who would have acted perfectly normally under ordinary circumstances. Occasionally, the "man in the street" could behave with a cruelty that would have been unthinkable in civilized society. An example is the mass execution at Hartberg in May 1945. A crowd standing three rows deep watched 13 bodies being hanged from lampposts and the only comment recorded, was: "What a pity to bury them in their good clothes!" One of the best characterizations of the Nazi regime was given by Arthur Seyss-Inquart during his trial at Nuremberg: "When a fanatical ideology is combined with an authoritarian government, there is no limit to the excesses that can occur." Seyss-Inquart, Hitler's faithful satrap in the Netherlands, knew what he was talking about.

A factor which must not be underestimated is the geographical position of Austria. Until November 1944 the war, at least the battle between opposing armies, was still taking place at a great distance. In France, Belgium, and Holland the population lived for years with the Allied armies outside the gates. The invasion was expected for a long time, and the Allied air forces were an ever-present reminder of the short distance from England. Liberation never seemed very far away, and minor actions—like the raids on Dieppe and Saint-Nazaire—kept hopes alive. By contrast, to the Austrians who longed for liberation as well as to the indifferent majority, the Allies seemed very far away. The air raids brought home to everyone the lesson that distance in modern war means very little, but this gave little encouragement. The raids were merely effective in destroying the morale of those who had believed in a German victory. In Germany their effect was quite different and even strengthened the will to fight to the finish.

The Austrians have rightly been criticized for lack of fighting spirit against their oppressors. As we have seen, armed resistance was limited to a few remote alpine areas. However, it must be admitted that even in France the actively fighting Maquis were numerically weak prior to the Allied invasion.[5] In Poland and Slovakia partisan warfare erupted when liberation seemed imminent and ended tragically in total disaster.

One additional reason for the cautious reaction of many citizens was the ultimate uncertainty concerning their political future. The mere restoration of the First Republic was no rallying point that created great enthusiasm. Many people who were anything but Nazis had bitter recollections of that period, especially the repressive era from 1933 to 1938. Thus, restoration of the status quo was a prospect that was preferable to German domination, but only moderately attractive. Some Austrian politicians-in-exile were even opposed to such a solution, but they were older men with obsolete ideas. The younger generation, especially the Socialist refugees in Sweden[6] were realists and clearly formulated their preference for a renewed independent republic. Still, quite a number of people had all sorts of misgivings concerning the restoration of a small

---

[5] The famous maquis de Glières, who fought pitched battles with the Germans and were wiped out in March 1944, numbered only about 500 men.
[6] Their spokesman was Bruno Kreisky, later chancellor.

state with a shattered economy. That this new Austrian Republic would 30 years later be one of the most healthy and prosperous countries in Europe was not to be foreseen.

However, few other alternatives actually existed. The Communists hoped for a Soviet Austria or, in later terminology, a People's Republic, but they were a very small, although dedicated, minority. A few of their functionaries, like the journalist Ernst Fischer and his attractive and courageous wife, had spent the war in the Soviet Union. On their return they found out that the Russian occupation was a very mixed blessing for their party. At the first election in November 1945 they only received 4 out of 165 seats in the new parliament. It is quite possible that the Communists would have done better had the Red Army never set foot in Austria. The realities of daily life under Soviet occupation quickly destroyed all effects of Communist propaganda.

Russia's new role in Eastern Europe also ended all illusions about a Danube Federation under a restored Hapsburg monarchy. The potential members of that federation, Hungary and Czechoslovakia, gradually turned into Soviet satellites, and Yugoslavia developed a dictatorship of its own. Plans for a Danube Federation, even including parts of Southern Germany, were under consideration until the Yalta Conference. In September 1944, Otto von Hapsburg was still taken seriously enough to be received by Winston Churchill in Quebec. But five months later at Yalta, that artificial federation was not even mentioned. It had been wrecked by political and military realities and was never revived.

Consequently, the Second Austrian Republic emerged as the only viable solution. Unlike its predecessor of 1918, it was not saddled with the heritage of the defunct Hapsburg monarchy, and the Allies were wise enough not to penalize Austria as a state for the sins of the Nazis. They concluded correctly that National Socialism in Austria was now a dead horse whose carrion would decompose in a natural manner. The cleaning-up they left to the Austrians without much interference. As in most formerly occupied countries, the "denazification" and legal procedures against war criminals dragged on for a long period of time. It cannot be said that the results were very satisfactory. With the passage of time the courts lost comprehension of the facts as they presented themselves in 1945. Over the years they seemed to lose their reality, and a number of undoubtedly guilty persons were acquitted by juries who seemed not to care or who were simply partial. To the younger generation it all was the residue of a strange, vague, fleeting past. There was no eagerness to punish anybody after such a long lapse of time.

On the positive side was the attitude of a number of Austrian statesmen who had greatly suffered under the German occupation but who never advocated revenge. Perhaps this was partly due to the experience of the past. The vindictiveness of 1934 and 1938 had created too much misery. Austrian politicians like Leopold Figl,[7] Adolf Schärf,[8] and Felix Hurdes[9] had been victims of the Nazi terror, and many others had spent years in prisons or concentration camps. They realized that all Austrians eventually had to coexist in a new Republic. Also, they knew their nation well. The majority had no reason to feel particularly proud of its attitude during the Nazi era and concluded that those bitter years were better forgotten. There were too many things one felt uncomfortable about. Besides, the atmosphere of the Cold War and a flood of postwar problems were not exactly conducive to soul-searching.

Thus, the doomsday propaganda of Hitler's last days proved a fraud. It merely led to a number of suicides. Among those who ended in this manner were the district leader of Lower Austria, Hugo Jury, the painter Carl Moll, and the poet Josef Weinheber.[10] Of the major Austrian war criminals, Kaltenbrunner, Seyss-Inquart, Rauter, and Eigruber were executed, but their trials were

---

[7] Federal Chancellor (1945–1953) and Foreign Minister (1953–1959).
[8] President of the Republic (1957–1965).
[9] Later Minister of Education and President of the National Assembly.
[10] Weinheber was one of the few talented men of letters who made common cause with the Nazis. His motives for suicide were doubtful.

held abroad. Most of the others got off with prison terms; some minor figures like Otto Skorzeny disappeared into exile. The rank and file—there were more than 500,000 of them—were briefly deprived of their civil rights but soon were pardoned. Many of them were small office-holders—so-called "bread Nazis"—who had joined the Party under pressure. Many profiteers and scoundrels got off very lightly. However, to create a large number of chronic malcontents would have been an even greater evil. As so often in history, political considerations proved stronger than demands for hard justice.

Austria's rebirth once and for all disproved the claim that a small independent state in Central Europe could not survive. Like many other small countries, it developed a healthy economy and sound democratic conditions when its existence ceased to be a matter of debate and conflict. Its tragic story—first as an unwanted byproduct of World War I, then as the country without a name —definitely belongs to the past.

BIBLIOGRAPHY

Andics, Hellmut. *Fünfzig Jahre unseres Lebens* [Fifty years of our lives]. Vienna: Molden, 1968.

Becker, H. *Österreichs Freiheitskampf* [Austria's struggle for freedom]. Vienna: Verlag der Freien Union der ÖVP, 1946.

Brook-Shepherd, Gordon. *Anschluss: The Rape of Austria.* London: Macmillan, 1963.

Buttinger, Joseph. *Am Beispiel Österreichs: Ein geschichtlicher Beitrag zur Krise der sozialistischen Bewegung* [The Austrian example: An historical contribution on the crisis of the Socialist movement]. Cologne: Verlag f. Politik u. Wirtschaft, 1953.

Danimann, Franz. *Finis Austriae.* Vienna: Europa, 1978.

Fein, E. *Die Steine reden* [The stones speak]. Vienna: Europa, 1975.

Flanner, K. *Widerstand im Gebiet von Wiener Neustadt* [Resistance in the district of Wiener Neustadt]. Vienna: Europa, 1973.

Fredberg, Awid. *Behind the Steel Wall.* London: Harrap, 1944.

Fuchs, Martin. *Showdown in Vienna.* New York: Putnam, 1939.

Gaiswinkler, A. *Sprung in die Freiheit* [Jump into freedom]. Vienna: Ried, 1947.

Gedye, G.E.R. *Die Bastionen fielen: Wie der Faschismus Wien und Prag überrannte* [The fallen bastions: How fascism overran Vienna and Prague]. Vienna: Danubia, 1948.

Grobauer, Franz Joseph. *Als Österreich zur Ostmark wurde* [When Austria became an eastern province]. Vienna: Selbstverlag Grobauer, 1977.

Jedlicka, Ludwig. *Der 20. Juli 1944 in Österreich* [July 20, 1944, in Austria]. Vienna: Herold, 1966.

Kalmar, Rudolf. *Zeit ohne Gnade* [Time without mercy]. Vienna: Schönbrunn, 1946.

Klusacek, Christine. *Die österreichische Freiheitsbewegung: Die Gruppe Roman Karl Scholz* [The Austrian freedom movement: The Roman Karl Scholz group]. Vienna: Europa, 1968.

Kühmayer, Ignaz C. *Auferstehung* [Resurrection]. Vienna: Dom, 1947.

Luza, Radomir. *Österreich und die großdeutsche Idee in der NS-Zeit* [Austria and the Pan-German idea in the National Socialist time]. Vienna: H. Böhlau Nachfolger, 1977.

Mikoletzky, Hans Leo. *Österreichische Zeitgeschichte* [Austrian history]. Vienna: Austria, 1969.

Molden, Fritz. *Fepolinski und Waschlapski auf dem berstenden Stern* [Fepolinski and Waschlapski on the exploding star]. Vienna: Molden, 1976.

Molden, Otto. *Der Ruf des Gewissens* [The call of conscience]. Vienna: Herold, 1970.

Moser, Jonny. *Die Judenverfolgung in Österreich* [Jewish persecution in Austria]. Vienna: Europa, 1966.

Muchitsch, M. *Die Partisanengruppe Leoben-Donawitz* [The Leoben-Donawitz partisan group]. Vienna: Europa, 1966.

Rauchensteiner, M. *Krieg in Österreich* [War in Austria], vol. 5. Vienna: Heeresgeschichtliches Museum, 1970.

Rauchensteiner, M. *1945. Entscheidung für Österreich* [1945. Decision for Austria]. Graz: Styria, 1975.

Rebhann, Fritz M. *Das braune Glück zu Wien.* Vienna: Herold, 1969.

Rebhann, Fritz M. *Finale in Wien* [Finale in Vienna]. Vienna: Herold, 1969.

Schausberger, Norbert. *Der Griff nach Österreich* [Grasping for Austria]. Vienna: Jugend (?) Volk, 1978.

Schuschnigg, Kurt von. *Im Kampf gegen Hitler* [In conflict with Hitler]. Vienna: Molden, 1969.

Spiegel, T. *Frauen und Mädchen im österreichischen Widerstand* [Women and girls in the Austrian Resistance]. Vienna: Europa, 1967.

Stadler, Karl R. *Österreich im Spiegel der NS-Akten* [Austria in the mirror of the NS (Nazi) documents]. Vienna: Herold, 1966.

Stadler, Karl R. *Austria.* London: Ernest Benn, 1970.

Steiner, Herbert. *Zum Tode verurteilt* [Condemned to death]. Vienna: Europa, 1964.

Steiner, Herbert. *Gestorben für Österreich* [Died for Austria]. Vienna: Europa, 1968.

Szesci, M. and Stadler, K. R. *Die NS-Justiz in Österreich* [The Nazi administration of justice in Austria]. Vienna: Herold, 1962.

Vogl, F. *Österreichische Eisenbahner im Widerstand* [Austrian railwaymen during the Resistance]. Vienna: Europa, 1968.

Wagner, Dietrich and Tomkowitz, Gerhard. *"Ein Volk, ein Reich, ein Führer!"* ["One people, one Reich, one leader!"] Munich: Piper, 1968.

Weinzierl, Erika. *Zu wenig Gerechte* [Too few just ones]. Graz: Styria, 1964.

Widerstand und Verfolgung in Wien [Resistance and persecution in

Vienna], vols. 2 and 3. Dokumentationsarchiv des österreichischen Widerstandes. Vienna: Österreichischer Bundesverlag, 1975.

Zahn, Gordon C. *In Solitary Witness: The Life and Death of Franz Jägerstätter.* New York: Holt, Rinehart & Winston, 1964.

Zernatto, Guido. *Die Wahrheit über Österreich* [The truth about Austria]. New York: Longmans, Green, 1938.

CHRONOLOGY

November 12, 1918	Proclamation of the Austrian Republic.
September 10, 1919	Treaty of Saint-Germain signed.
September 11, 1930	Last general election in Austria before the *Anschluss.*
May 24, 1931	Serious bank crisis, *Kreditanstalt* collapses.
May 4, 1932	Dollfuss becomes Chancellor.
January 30, 1933	Hitler becomes German Chancellor.
March 7, 1933	Dollfuss begins to govern without parliament.
June 19, 1933	NSDAP banned in Austria.
February 12, 1934	Civil war breaks out in Austria.
February 15, 1934	Socialist resistance collapses.
July 25, 1934	Nazi putsch in Austria, Dollfuss assassinated.
July 29, 1934	Schuschnigg becomes Chancellor.
October 3, 1935	Mussolini invades Ethiopia.
March 7, 1936	Occupation of the Rhineland.
July 11, 1936	Austro-German agreement.
February 12, 1938	Conference between Hitler and Schuschnigg in Berchtesgaden.
March 12, 1938	German troops invade Austria.
March 13, 1938	Hitler declares fusion of Austria with the Reich.
September 29, 1938	Munich Conference on Czechoslovakia.
March 15, 1939	Hitler annexes Czechoslovakia.
August 23, 1939	German-Soviet nonaggression treaty signed.
September 1, 1939	German invasion of Poland.
September 3, 1939	Britain and France declare war on Germany.
September 28, 1939	War in Poland ends.
April 9, 1940	Denmark and Norway invaded.
May 10, 1940	German offensive in the Low Countries and Ardennes.
June 22, 1940	Armistice of Compiègne; France surrenders.
July 7, 1940	Schirach becomes district leader of Vienna.

April 6, 1941	Germans invade Yugoslavia and Greece.
June 22, 1941	Germans attack Soviet Union.
December 6, 1941	Russian counter-offensive near Moscow.
December 7, 1941	Japanese attack on Pearl Harbor.
December 10, 1941	Germany declares war on the US.
July 17, 1942	Germans advance against Stalingrad.
November 4, 1942	British victory at El Alamein.
November 8, 1942	Allied landing in North Africa.
February 2, 1943	Germans surrender at Stalingrad.
May 13, 1943	Axis troops in Tunis surrender.
June 30, 1943	Allied landings in Sicily.
July 25, 1943	Mussolini deposed.
August 13, 1943	First air raid on Wiener Neustadt.
September 3, 1943	Italian surrender signed.
November 1, 1943	Allied declaration on Austria's independence.
March 19, 1944	Germans occupy Hungary.
June 6, 1944	Allied invasion of Normandy.
July 20, 1944	Military putsch against Hitler fails.
August 23, 1944	Romania joins the Allies.
August 25, 1944	Paris liberated.
December 16, 1944	Rundstedt's offensive in Belgium.
February 4, 1945	Three-power conference at Yalta.
February 13, 1945	Russians take Budapest.
March 23, 1945	Allies cross the Rhine.
March 28, 1945	Russians cross Austrian border.
April 2, 1945	Vienna declared fortress area.
April 13, 1945	Vienna in Russian hands.
April 27, 1945	Provisional Austrian government is established.
April 29, 1945	Germans surrender in Italy.
May 3, 1945	Innsbruck liberated.
May 7, 1945	Germany's unconditional surrender to Allies.
May 9, 1945	End of World War II in Europe.

INDEX

Mo: :   .